CONTENTS ✍ **W9-BIR-307**

Chapters

AIRLINE PILOT INTERVIEWS

HOW YOU CAN SUCCEED IN GETTING HIRED

By IRV JASINSKI

Published By: CAREER ADVANCEMENT PUBLICATIONS
Post Office Box 271409
Escondido, CA 92027 U.S.A.

Printed in the United States of America
Library of Congress Catalog Card Number: 87-70680
ISBN-0-942195-01-9 Softcover

AIRLINE PILOT INTERVIEWS

HOW YOU CAN SUCCEED
IN GETTING HIRED

IRV JASINSKI
Pilot Interview Coach

Copyright 1987

Career Advancement Publications
Escondido, California

DEDICATED TO LEE . . . My Wife, Best Friend, And Most Important Person In My Life

"Yep! I'm gonna like flying with you guys!"

WHY SHOULD YOU READ THIS BOOK?

The competition among pilot applicants for airline pilot jobs is more intense and unique than in any other profession. Getting hired depends on more than your technical qualifications: hours, ratings, flight skills, and aircraft flown. These are tools that can open the door for your interview. From that point on, everything depends on how you present your flight and personal credentials and how you react under the pressure of an intense interview. Your performance during the interview is crucial to the decision of whether you or someone else will be selected.

This book concentrates on showing you how to prepare an impressive pilot resume and employment package, how to obtain the interviews you want, and how to present yourself in the most effective, professional manner during an interview.

The book is written by a person who has first-hand experience in hiring airline pilots for a major carrier. It clears up many misconceptions that pilot applicants have about the whole screening, selection, and hiring process. If you are a pilot preparing for an upcoming interview for a better flying job, you will find the techniques and information in this book will greatly enhance your chances of getting hired. You will want to keep this book nearby as a handy reference to turn to again and again as you go through the various phases of your job search and interview preparation.

After the hundreds of hours and thousands of dollars you have invested to get this far along in your flight career, doesn't it seem prudent to take this additional step in learning how to present your qualifications and *yourself* during that crucial interview, when just one or two seemingly insignificant mistakes can jeopardize your future?

WHO IS IRV JASINSKI?

Irv Jasinski is head of Airline Pilot Employment Advisors (APEA), and for several years he has been coaching pilots in how to apply effective interviewing techniques. During his coaching sessions, he conducts mock interviews that are geared to the particular airline that will be interviewing the pilot applicant. He covers questions asked by the Personnel Department, Flight Department, physician, and psychologist, and he critiques the answers given by the applicant . . . pointing out all of the ways the applicant can make a better impression. Irv's advertisements geared to pilot applicants appear regularly in the Future Aviation Professionals of America magazine.

In response to requests from pilots throughout the country, Irv has written this book. Drawing upon his extensive coaching and hiring experience, he discusses employment preparation approaches and many interviewing practices, techniques, hints, and insights that have helped many pilots get hired by the airlines.

Irv spent ten years with Flying Tiger Line as their Manager of Employment and Pilot Recruitment. He personally screened, interviewed, assessed, and selected hundreds of their pilots. He designed the airline's employment application, screening procedures, and the screening and interviewing methods of the Pilot Review Board. He developed many of the questions pilots are asked, chose the factors to be considered in assessing Flight Officer job candidates, and played a key role in the final selection process. He interacted closely with the hiring staffs of many airlines, comparing notes on their reasons for hiring or not hiring pilot candidates. He speaks openly and candidly on these matters throughout the book.

While he was with Flying Tigers, Irv taught courses in interviewing techniques and career development at University of California Extension locations throughout the state.

As head of APEA, he has conducted seminars in effective job search and applicant interviewing techniques at flight schools and in major cities throughout the country. Irv holds a Bachelor Degree in psychology/personnel/business management, and he has taken many advanced state-of-the-art courses in these fields and in study areas that concentrate on presentation skills for career enhancement.

HOW DO YOU "SCORE" WITH THE AIRLINES?

This book was written to help you gain more insight into the entire airline screening and evaluation process—to tell you what to do and not do to score points and increase your chances of getting hired. It should cause you to think more in depth about yourself and how you can present all that you have going for you in the best possible manner. You will be surprised when you learn how many things you do have going for you. On the other hand, you may find that what you thought were the right things to do during an interview might have already cost you some excellent flight career opportunities. You will learn better ways of approaching your interview, deciding what to say, how to say it, and when to say it. You will be more prepared for your interviews and more relaxed and confident when they happen.

If you were to look at two stacks of pilot resumes, one of which represented applicants who were hired by the airlines and the other of applicants not hired, you probably wouldn't be able to tell them apart. The candidates in both stacks would appear to be qualified technically. Perhaps some would not have been hired because of the airline's concern about the results of their medical examination, simulator check, or written tests. However, most of those who were turned down actually failed somewhere in their interviews. They just didn't score for some reason with the Personnel Department, the Flight Department, the physician, the psychologist, or with someone else in management. There could have been a number of things that went wrong or just one thing in particular that blew their chance for a great career. They may be aware of what happened or they may be at a total loss to determine or understand what it was and when it happened. Without further insight or advice, they might well repeat the same mistakes in future interviews.

On the surface, an interview may seem like "a piece of cake." Underneath, there are many wheels and gears turning—weighing this and that, consciously and subconsciously. Some airline interviewers play the role of both interviewer and interrogator. They can be friendly and easy to talk to at certain times during the session; at other times, they can be quite blunt and irritating as they probe the applicant's background looking for hidden problem areas.

Let's clear up some misconceptions that exist among pilots trying to get on with the airlines. One is: "My getting hired or rejected will be based primarily on my flight qualifications. Those who have the heaviest technical qualifications get the jobs." Actually, your flight qualifications are the primary reasons you will be called in for an interview—but from that point on, getting hired depends on how well you perform in the interviewing process and throughout all of the other phases of pilot applicant assessment. If, in fact, your qualifications spoke for themselves, the airlines would not have to test and interview you. They could just run your qualifications through the computer and send you an offer or a rejection.

Here are two more misconceptions: "They will have to prove to me that I'm not qualified" and "They will have to find out what's wrong with me to turn me down." On the contrary, you will have to prove to them that you are well qualified, and they will be determined to find out what's right with you before they will consider hiring you. It's a lot like winning a football game. You go into the game with no points on the board, and your objective is to make enough points to win. If you play too defensive a game, the other team can beat you with a three-point field goal. Airline interviews can be approached in the same way: What does it take to win this game? Throughout the interview, you are continuously being assessed as you make points, fail to make points, or even lose points. You have to make as many points as possible in your interview to win a Flight Officer job. Your game must be played offensively all the way. If you sit back, speak as little as you think is necessary to answer questions, and put only minimum effort into trying to prove to those interviewing you that you are more capable and qualified than the other candidates, then you are not going to be hired. It's that simple! Just a point or two difference between you and another candidate can determine who wins the game—who gets the job.

THEY WANT A PROFICIENT PILOT

There are two things that the airlines look for primarily in a pilot candidate: a very technically proficient pilot and a very impressive individual. In this chapter, we'll discuss your technical proficiency. Chapter 3 covers your impressiveness as an individual.

Are you a technically proficient pilot? How well have you planned and followed through on your education, flight training, and flight experience? What was the quality of your flight training? How strong are your flight skills and techniques? How well will you perform in this airline's simulator? How well will you perform on the line? How much military or commuter and/or corporate flying experience do you have? Will your overall record and interview presentation project an image of professional airmanship?

In the past, a strong preference was given to military flight experience over civilian flight experience. Today, both types of experience are considered valuable. Both have produced excellent airline pilots. Experience that reflects disciplined training and day and night flying in bad weather is sought by the airlines, whether this experience is obtained from military or civilian activity.

Let's boil it down to specific flight credentials. In terms of total flight time, when you have obtained 1,500 hours, you have entered the ball park with most airlines. Some airlines will occasionally consider candidates with as few as 500 total flight hours for a Flight Engineer position. This will vary, depending on how many pilots they need, how soon they need them, and the availability of high-time pilot candidates. When it comes to pilot-in-command time and heavy jet time, the more the better. More credit is given to multi-engine time than single-engine time. Fixed-wing time is given preference over rotary-wing time . . . turbo-prop over reciprocating . . . jet over turbo-prop.

An ATP ticket throws a lot of weight. To the airlines it represents a professional pilot, just as having a CPA represents a professional accountant.

Acquiring an A Type rating that is applicable to the airline's fleet will significantly increase your candidate qualifications.

The FE Writtens are a must if you are applying for a Flight Engineer position. Interviewers look for high scores and expect the more seasoned pilot candidates to score high. If you scored over 90, note it in your resume following "FE Writtens." During an interview, you could be asked if you can recall what questions you missed on your FE Writtens and if you now know the correct answers. Give it some thought before your interview.

The FE rating in itself is given a significant amount of credit in the assessment process, especially if you obtained your rating in the same aircraft flown by the airline to which you are applying. If at all possible, gear your rating to those airlines for whom you most want to fly. In some cases, this can save the airlines thousands of dollars in training costs in not having to put you through their entire ground-training program. At the least, it significantly increases the probability of your successfully completing their FE-training program. It also points out to them that you were willing to invest a great amount of your money, time, and effort toward advancing your career.

You are expected to have a First-Class FAA Medical, with no restrictions. Ideally, they want your vision to be 20/20 uncorrected in both eyes. However, many carriers will consider candidates with vision limitations beyond that level, providing it is correctable to 20/20.

Having some flight instructor experience is to your advantage, but preferably not more than one-third of your total flight time. It is thought of as dual pilot experience and reflects excellent pilot-to-pilot communication skills. Two-pilot cockpit time is highly valued by many airlines. Your desire to flight instruct, however, should never be expressed in an interview as being more important than your desire to "fly the line."

The prime age range of pilots hired is approximately 25 to 35, but there has been a more open-minded attitude on the part of the airlines concerning age latitude. Greater consideration is being given to the quality and overall caliber of the pilot candidate. Although "return on investment" from an age viewpoint is a very important consideration, it is no longer just a matter of how many remaining years a pilot will have to fly for the airline but how effective that pilot will be in all respects throughout his or her employment with the airline. More and more candidates above and below the prime age range are being hired because they project the image of a quality pilot.

In terms of formal education, first preference is given to candidates having a Bachelor degree. Second preference is given to those with an Associate degree. Third consideration goes to those having one or two years of college. Greater latitude is given to the field of study as well. In the past, heavy emphasis was placed upon Aviation Engineering fields. Today, the door has opened wider to accept most fields of study from accredited colleges and universities. A field of study, however, which is directly aviation-related, technical, or in management is certainly desirable from the airline's perspective. Degrees in the business and psychological fields are considered advantageous because many airlines feel that to be successful in today's highly competitive aviation atmosphere, a Flight Officer must be more than a technically qualified pilot. During lean times, you may have to perform in a non-flying position in order to avoid being furloughed. Even if it's temporary, you are expected to perform well in every position to which you are assigned. It is also beneficial for you to have knowledge of and take interest in the business end of the airline and to successfully interact with all types and levels of people—both flight and non-flight within and outside the company. Being able to do this increases your effectiveness and value to the company. Your formal education can play a significant part in making this happen.

When it comes to grades, the airlines expect you to have an overall college grade average of at least C plus—preferably much higher. Candidates with low grade-point averages must do a solid job of convincing the interviewers that their grade average in college doesn't truly reflect their learning ability. During the interview, reference can be made to the better grades attained during flight-school training and while obtaining advanced ratings. Or perhaps upward job progression over the years can be cited as evidence of the learning ability necessary to quickly grasp new job assignments. Airline management must feel assured that you are smart enough to successfully complete their flight-training program. Otherwise you will not be hired.

All airlines desire candidates with strong mechanical aptitude. You should bring this aptitude out in the interview. For example, you might mention that you maintain your own automobile, have a small machine shop, work with wood or metal, etc.

Staying current is very important. Airline flight management is interested primarily in pilots who are and have been actively flying, working on ratings, or flight instructing; that is, doing something directly related to flight career progress. They have serious reservations about pilot candidates who have entered a field of work unrelated to flying and have earned an impressive income in that field. They will question whether such a candidate is seriously interested in a long-range career as a pilot with their airline. Consider the large number of carriers that have a two-tier or similar pay structure for pilots. They prefer to weed out candidates who are in the flying profession mainly for the "big bucks," without a sincere desire to fly.

As you attain additional qualifications that increase your technical proficiency, send an update letter to the airline's personnel manager, basically saying:

> "I am a Flight Officer candidate with your airline. Please update my . . . (hours, ratings, equipment, employment record, education, etc.) to reflect (the change). I am continuing to increase my pilot skills and qualifications and anxiously await hearing from you."

"TIME FOR A BREAK" QUIZ . . .

Try connecting all nine cities with only four straight, continuous lines (no back tracking).

LOS ANGELES   LAS VEGAS   DENVER

•   •   •

KANSAS CITY   CHICAGO   DETROIT

•   •   •

CLEVELAND   BUFFALO   NEW YORK

•   •   •

Give up? Turn to the next page.

ANSWER TO "TIME FOR A BREAK" QUIZ...

LOS ANGELES   LAS VEGAS   DENVER

KANSAS CITY   CHICAGO   DETROIT

CLEVELAND   BUFFALO   NEW YORK

Simple, isn't it? Why don't most of us come up with the answer on our first approach? We think that we must somehow solve the problem within the square area—the corners of which are Los Angeles, Denver, Cleveland, and New York.

It is only when we go outside our self-restricted square that we can solve the problem. Applying this same thought process to the challenge of getting an airline pilot job offer, we could consider the square area as that encompassed by flight hours, ratings, certificates, aircraft flown, education, and training. The area beyond the square into which we must extend ourselves in order to attain our goal can be thought of as qualitative attributes—such as love of flying, safety consciousness, leadership, professionalism, attitude, personality, values, etc.

Most of us have learned to solve our problems using the same tools over and over, because they have always worked for us. When we come to a new problem that our old tools don't seem capable of solving, it's time to look elsewhere for new tools. Relating this to our profession, we can't afford to lose opportunities for flight career advancement through stubbornly adhering to old tools that have worked in the past. We shouldn't bang our heads against the wall determined that all the right answers lie in front of us, as they always have, when we need to look all around us. During the interview, we must possess and display those attributes both within and outside the square (quantitative and qualitative) in the most favorable light possible.

"I'm ready when you are!"

THEY WANT AN IMPRESSIVE INDIVIDUAL

Along with technical proficiency, the most important attribute the airlines seek in a pilot candidate is personal impressiveness. Many interviewers feel that your effectiveness on the job is primarily tied in with your personality, character, traits, values, etc.

One of the most important ingredients necessary to build an impressive personal image, in the opinion of many flight, personnel, and management people, is a *strong, positive attitude*. Do you view a new and complex situation as an opportunity for improvement or as an unwanted problem? Do you display a positive attitude in your approach and interaction with everyone you work with, day in and day out?

Is your attitude really that important? Well, consider this statement, which was made recently by a major airline flight executive: "I can 'give some' on a pilot candidate who doesn't have heavy flight time or who perhaps didn't do as well as he or she should have in his or her grades in college, but I'll be damned if I will give one inch to *any* candidate who doesn't have a good attitude! We can train and retrain a pilot in areas of flight knowledge much easier than we can change that pilot's attitude. We are *not* in the business of changing people's attitudes. It's too difficult and time consuming! We have to accept pilots as we view them—in the attitude which they reflect to us in every aspect of their contact with our airline, throughout our whole pilot assessment process. That attitude has to be good!"

A pure love of flying is considered by many airline managers and psychologists as crucial to establishing a highly successful career as a Flight Officer. It correlates closely with staying current and doing your best at what you most enjoy. It may well be the key reason why some airline pilots are more impressive in their performance out on the line than others who are more technically qualified. The airlines would like to feel that the pilot candidate whom they have chosen has a desire to fly that is greater than any other desire for any other type of job. If that pilot couldn't fly for medical reasons, he or she would still want a job related to flying within the airline industry. This desire to fly is the basic motivation and foundation upon which a person applies all of his or her energies, abilities, and potentials toward becoming a better and better pilot in every respect. It nurtures a very strong pride in being a pilot and being able to earn a living doing something so enjoyable . . . flying!

A strong, safety-conscious attitude which permeates everything you do as a pilot is considered by many Flight Department heads as the most important attribute you can possess. They look for evidence of such an attitude in every way possible: record of accidents and incidents; feedback from prior employers on your display of safety consciousness; and your initiative in discussing safety during your interview, pointing out that it is one of your major strengths. How do you intend to sell yourself in this respect?

Captain potential is of vital importance to the airlines. Employment and Flight Department Managers are, in reality, evaluating you primarily from the perspective of how successful you will be in the future as a Captain, if hired, rather than for the immediate opening (Second or First Officer). They look for signs of Captain potential in your flight experience and past record of leadership accomplishments in your various job responsibilities, training, schooling, etc., and in the way you handle yourself during the interview—how you act, what you say, and how you say it. Let them know that you have a strong desire to become a Captain with them and will make every effort to earn that position by establishing an impressive performance record as a Second Officer and First Officer with their airline.

The airlines also look for individuals who can perform well under stress and pressure. When the going gets rough a pilot must not become frustrated, defensive, or overreactive to situations. In a flight emergency, this could be disastrous. Stress situations and stress producing questions may be interjected throughout the interview to observe how you respond to pressure. Some interviewers can be very subtle in their approach, others quite direct. For example, you could be asked if you have ever smoked marijuana. Should you answer no, the interviewer will continue to question you on the same issue to note if you lose your cool or change your story, which will jeopardize your credibility. We will discuss many of these stress situations and questions later when we concentrate on the interview itself.

The airlines are looking for a strong team-oriented type of person—someone who can get along very well with the other crew members in the cockpit and in the cabin, as well as on layovers. They want a pilot who is crew-concept oriented, placing team success above individual recognition, helping and backing up a fellow crew member in every way possible. In conversation, team-oriented people often make reference to we, our and us. Those not team oriented frequently identify with I, me, and mine. If something accomplished was a team effort, "we" should be used. If it was principally the result of your achievements and attributes, then "I" is appropriate. Interviewers watch for these identifying signs during the interview and in written presentations (cover letters, correspondence, etc.).

A strong learning ability is an important asset. It helps to assure flight managers that you can successfully complete their airline's training and recurrent training programs. Your past grades and class standings are one indicator of this. The way you adapt to the interview itself also reflects your learning ability. Do you pick up quickly on the mood of the interviewers, understand their questions, and gain insight into what they are looking for? Do you perceive how much time they are likely to spend on each question, and learn when it's time for you to stop talking?

Airlines want a pilot who looks, acts, dresses, and speaks professionally on and off duty; who handles people and situations in a professional manner; and who creates a good public image. In what ways do you project professionalism and how can you improve your professional image?

Self-confidence is another highly desired trait. Do you project it throughout the interview? Do you seem proud of what you have accomplished and project confidence that you will succeed if given the opportunity to fly for them?

Flight Managers look for evidence of adaptability and flexibility. They would like to believe they are hiring someone who can successfully adjust and adapt to any situation, whether a less desirable domicile or trip, an unexpected furlough, or a family crisis. They seek individuals who can handle frustrations and who can readily adapt to new schedules, aircraft, routes, people, places, things, and ideas.

Airlines also want well-rounded, personable individuals. This ties in closely with attitude, adaptability, and flexibility. Pilots have to interact daily with many other employees within and outside the Flight Department, including the terminal management staff, gate and ticket counter personnel, ground crews, flight and crew schedulers, secretaries, people in operations, engineering, sales, personnel, and other departments. The interviewer wants to know how compatible and conversant you would be in discussions (both work and non-work related) with fellow employees. Can you take the lead at times? Would you be considered an interesting, diversified, stimulating person to talk to, or someone narrow in interests who shows little desire to discuss topics outside of flying? Do you listen attentively to others when they are speaking? When people enjoy conversing with you on any subject, they will extend themselves to help you and do things for you which go beyond their normal job responsibilities. They will make an extra effort to please you because you have developed a strong mutual rapport with each of them.

A factor that has a significant bearing upon a pilot's total contribution and worth to the airline is influence over other people. Some people make others around them feel uncomfortable for some reason. If you convey that feeling in an interview, it could kill your chance of getting hired. A Captain interviewing Flight Officer applicants will not recommend someone whom he or she would not personally be at ease with during a trip or layover. You have only so much ability and potential, but your strong, positive influence over others is an added force that can do more for the company than you could do alone. You can help others apply their abilities more effectively and recognize the full latitude of their potentials. When others observe you, do you appear enthusiastic about yourself, the airline, and the future? Are you an example of a person who enjoys coming to work? Do you stimulate and inspire others? This ability to influence both individual and team performance in many positive ways is very difficult to measure, yet we all recognize it when we spot it in certain people. For someone who is a Captain, it is an extremely important asset, crucial to effective crew interaction. Airlines seek it in Flight Officer candidates. You must directly or indirectly display your share of it in your interviews.

The ability to communicate effectively can add many points to your total score. How well do you convey what you are trying to say to interviewers in your choice of words, use of your voice, facial expressions, etc.? Are your answers and statements clear and concise? Could you further expand your vocabulary, choose more descriptive words in answering questions, and more effectively control the volume, pitch, and speed of your voice? Do you under or over communicate? Are you easily understood? How do you sound to your peers and friends? Are you impressive?

Having a good sense of humor contributes a great deal to achieving a successful flight career. Do you display signs of it during the interview? While the interviewers are kidding one another or you and observing your reaction, are you smiling or looking at them as though they had dropped all their marbles? Can you take kidding and be able to laugh at yourself? One of the most effective methods of preventing a heated discussion from turning into an argument is to introduce humor. It's difficult to become angry with someone who has just said something funny to you. Out on the flight line, having a good sense of humor can help to establish many lasting friendships, as well as prevent run-ins with other company personnel. People are more comfortable and at ease around you. It really counts.

The airlines are also seeking pilot candidates who are past, present, and future oriented. During an interview, do you talk primarily about what you have accomplished and relatively little about what you are currently accomplishing? On the other hand, do you do an impressive job of relating to your past and present achievements but fail to bring out any future plans to improve yourself as a pilot and as an individual? Are you goal oriented? You must remember that the ultimate hiring decision rests upon the extent to which the airlines view you as being successful in the future as a Captain with their airline! Certainly your past and present achievements and attitude will strongly influence your future successes. In addition, however, the airlines want some further indication and insight from you as to what you intend to do in the future. They want assurance that you will be successful with them if they hire you.

We will discuss appropriate dress, appearance, personality, speaking and writing skills, etc., in the chapters ahead.

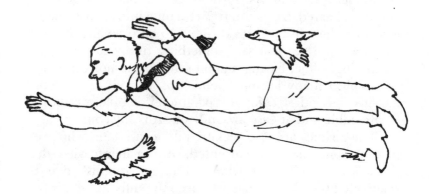

"Just love to fly!"

WHAT YOU SHOULD KNOW ABOUT THE AIRLINES

You are very likely to be asked early in your interview, "How much do you know about our airline? Why would you rather fly for us than one of the other carriers?" You should be prepared to provide some specific answers to these questions. The interviewer wants to know that you are interested enough in this specific airline to have taken the time to find out from a number of people and a variety of sources as much as you possibly could about the airline, from a number of perspectives. (A comprehensive list of interview questions asked, by subject area, is provided in Chapter 16.)

Your knowledge of this particular airline and other airlines also helps you to determine which one would be most compatible with your personal and flight career interests, needs, and goals. What type of information should you look for? What are the factors by which you can assess one airline against the others? These are some of the things you should investigate:

1. Overall reputation among pilots.
2. Caliber of the people you will be flying and working with—the general atmosphere.
3. Individual treatment and recognition.

4. Caliber and reputation of their top management in the aviation and business world.
5. Likelihood of an unwanted takeover or merger.
6. Financial status.
7. Equity-to-debt ratio.
8. Cash reserves, total assets, and business outlook.
9. Expansion plans.
10. Past track record.
11. Time it takes to upgrade from Flight Engineer to First Officer, to Captain.
12. Salary structure and progression.
13. Employee benefits.
14. Probability of being furloughed periodically and length of time.
15. Whether it is predominately a passenger or cargo carrier.
16. Types of aircraft flown—loaned, leased, or purchased.
17. Size of fleet.
18. Routes, trips, and layovers.
19. Domiciles.
20. Pass and jump seat privileges.
21. Retirement programs.

Do not bring up salary, benefits, furloughing, domiciles desired, etc., in the interview. You don't want to present a "What can you do for me" attitude.

Ask yourself these questions: "Will I feel challenged as a professional Flight Officer and thoroughly enjoy my daily interactions with personnel on all levels? Is this the type of airline with which I want to identify myself for the next 25 to 35 years?"

On a sheet of paper write across the sheet the names of the airlines that appeal to you most. Then list all the factors which mean the most to you down the left-hand side of the sheet. Score each airline on each factor—from zero to ten (highest) and note this on a scratch sheet of paper. Place a *weighted value* of importance to you on each factor being considered—from zero to ten, and note this next to the factor score. Multiply each *factor score* earned for each airline by the weighted value you assigned to that factor to get the total points. Record the total points earned for each factor under the name of each airline listed, across from that factor. Now add up this column of points earned for that airline. Rank the airlines in order by total points earned. The airline scoring the greatest number of points goes on top. Which are your top three airlines? You may be surprised at the results. Devote the majority of your search efforts to those airlines.

How do you get information on each of the airlines? There are a number of sources, including these:

1. Future Aviation Professionals of America (FAPA), World Aviation Directory, Standard and Poors, Moody, Aviation Week and Space Technology, Aviation Daily, Flight International, Airline Pilot, Air Transport World, The Wall Street Journal, Forbes, Business Week, Airline Executive, Business/Commercial Aviation, Commuter Air, Professional Pilot, Flight Crew, Readers Guide To Periodical Literature.
2. Annual reports issued by the Public Relations Department of each airline.
3. Airline's advertisements, newspapers, newsletters, promotional brochures, and other handout materials.
4. Flight and ground schools.
5. College and university libraries and placement departments.
6. Pilots (active and retired) and other airline employees who are up-to-date in knowing how fast pilots are being upgraded and what is happening at their airline and others as well.

The more of these sources, and others, that you pursue, the more confident will be your decision about which airlines you want to work for; and the more impressive you will be during an interview.

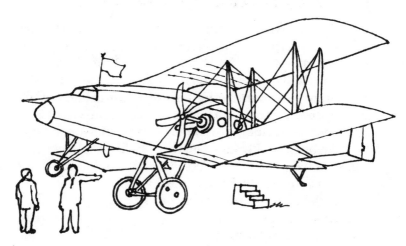

"We picked it up for our short-haul, over-night, small package delivery."

CHAPTER 5

HOW TO PREPARE A PROFESSIONAL RESUME/ EMPLOYMENT PACKAGE

At this point, you are ready to present yourself to the airlines on paper. You certainly want to express yourself as clearly and candidly as possible in everything you submit. Your Employment Package should consist of:

1. Cover Letter or Broadcast Letter.
2. Employment Application.
3. Resume.
4. Flight Data Form.
5. Supporting Documents.

COVER LETTER OR BROADCAST LETTER

The Cover or Broadcast Letter serves as an introduction to your Employment Package. It should be written in a conversational style, using the same words you normally use in a one-on-one conversation.

A Cover Letter makes a brief statement or two about your intentions and the materials you are submitting. Essentially, it says:

"I am applying for a Flight Officer position with your airline. Enclosed is my completed Employment Application, Flight Data Form, Resume, and supporting documents. I look forward to the opportunity of presenting my qualifications directly to you in an interview."

A Broadcast Letter is actually a Cover Letter that goes one step further. It points out the highlights of your flight background, such as total flight hours, an ATP, an FE rating in . . . (aircraft), . . . (hours) jet time, A Type rating in a . . . (aircraft), . . . (hours) pilot-in-command time, a flight instructor's rating, and your college degree and major (if applicable to your aviation career). It is primarily a snapshot of your Resume to whet the reader's appetite to read through your entire Employment Package. Emphasis is placed upon your most meaningful technical flight qualifications. Should the particular airline you are addressing show strong preference for certain ratings, equipment exposure, or type of flying experience, be certain to highlight in your letter the fact that you possess them, if such be the case. The Broadcast Letter gives the reader an immediate candid view of your flight expertise. It may prompt the reader to review your Employment Package more thoroughly than others, especially if there are stacks to be screened in a limited period of time. The screener can't pick up your Employment Package and begin reading your Broadcast Letter without immediately becoming aware of your primary flight achievements.

EMPLOYMENT APPLICATION

Your Employment Application is the company's tool to control and direct you in telling them what they want to know about you. The Resume, on the other hand, is your tool and enables you to tell the company only what you want it to know about you. You should type (preferably) or print your statements on the Employment Application. It is too difficult for interviewers to read the handwriting of most pilot candidates.

Your Employment Application is the airline's official employment record (legal document) for every job applicant. Falsification of statements on the Employment Application, rather than on the Resume, have been grounds for withdrawal of an offer of employment, and even termination of employment after hire. Practice filling out a copy of the blank application before submitting a final copy.

Complete your Employment Application in a professional manner. If any of the questions on the application do not pertain to you or your background, type or print N/A (not applicable). Do not make frequent remarks such as "see Resume" or "see enclosures"—interviewers don't enjoy having to jump back and forth between your Employment Application and other enclosures to piece together your qualifications. An exception to this is when your reason for leaving college, dropping out of a training program, or quitting a particular job requires some explanation. Put "To Be Discussed" where you are asked the reason for leaving a job and where you note that you dropped out of college or a training program. Print small, if you need to, in order to include everything important, rather than half-answer the questions for lack of space. Elaborate on answers that help bring out your strong points and be brief on those that point out areas of weakness. Submit a newly completed application whenever the original one becomes outdated through numerous updates. Keep your own file copy of each completed application you have submitted.

RESUME

Your Resume is considered by many hiring managers as the most important document in your Employment Package. It condenses the most important aspects of your completed Employment Application and Flight Data form. Many interviewers decide whom to call in for an interview after reviewing stacks of Resumes. Some interviewers refer to the Resume during the interview more than the Employment Application because just about everything they need to know is on one piece of paper. The Resume represents you, since you designed and developed it. It reflects you in every way. You chose what to include and what to leave out. It is your image on paper. Do you look well organized and professional? Will the reader want to meet you in person?

Lay out your Resume as impressively as you can. It should be one page long, if at all possible, and typed on an electric typewriter or typeset. Many word processors do an excellent job as well. Use high-quality, textured paper. Beige, light blue, or gray are preferred colors. Do not reproduce your Resume on a copying machine—you don't want fade out on certain letters or specks of black. Have a local printer produce them for you. Their equipment is designed for professional-looking copies.

Should you include a photograph? In general, the answer is no. Many candidates may unawaringly convey an image of being overweight, needing a haircut, appearing much younger or older than they might want to, or project a facial expression that is negatively misinterpreted by the viewer (a silly grin or an uptight look). Your photograph might instantly remind the person screening Employment Packages of someone he or she dislikes. Why chance it? If, however, that airline has an active Affirmative Action Program and you are a minority or female, a photograph might be to your advantage. If you make this decision, have the photograph taken at a professional studio.

The most effective Resumes are meaty, meaningful, well laid out, crisp, concise, and clear. There should not be any unnecessary words or statements. Tell the airlines what they need to know about you, not what would be nice to know about you. If what you plan to include in your Resume has a definite purpose geared to selling yourself, then put it in.

Let's develop an effective Resume, following the most appropriate sequence of major areas.

"Which 'winner' should I send?"

Heading

First of all, you don't have to state "Resume" at the top of the page—they will know what it is from the format and layout. Place your full name, address and phone number(s) at or near the center and top of the page. (Some candidates date their Resume. Unless you revise it frequently, this is not recommended.) You should provide more than one phone number (home and message) so that a phone message from the airlines will reach you within a few hours, at the most, any day of the week. Don't be skipped over for an interview opportunity in favor of another candidate who made it his or her business to ensure being reached immediately. Use an automatic phone answering/recording unit. It is well worth the investment when you consider the results at stake.

Position

This first major area should be capitalized [as should the letters of all the major headings you will use] and placed to the far-left margin of the page, followed by the statement "Flight Officer for . . . (name of airline)"—tailored to the top five airlines on your airline assessment list. Don't make your headings too wordy and open ended. Make a brief to the point statement.

Flight Qualifications

Categorize all your flight credentials in this area of your Resume as follows:

1. *Flight Time*
   Be certain to cover all significant time breakdowns, such as Pilot-in-Command (PIC), Multi-Engine, Instrument, Turbo-Prop, and Turbo-Jet. Include instructor hours if they represent less than a third of your total hours.

Military pilots can use the civilian approach to logging time—block out to block in, or add a conversion factor of an additional 0.2 hour for each sortie as a fighter pilot and even more (in your judgment) for heavy equipment reflecting longer taxi times. Flight time is measured from the time the aircraft moves under its own power for flight to the time it stops moving and comes to a standstill at the next point of landing.

Some pilots have their Resumes reproduced with the time left off and fill it in as they submit or update their Resumes. Unless it is the same exact print size, typeface, and heaviness this approach is not recommended.

Don't round off your time to larger whole numbers (2000, 2025, 2050). They may think you are not only hedging on your time by rounding off upwards but in other areas of your Resume as well.

2. *Aircraft Flown*

   List all aircraft flown, starting with those that you feel would be of the most value to the airlines. Heavier and jet aircraft should be listed first.

3. *Ratings & Certificates*

   Place your ATP, Type Ratings, and FE Tickets at the top of your list. They carry a great deal of weight when it comes to flying with the airlines. If you have an A & P License, list it also. It reflects a strong knowledge of aircraft systems, essential to a Flight Engineer's role in monitoring flight systems. If your vision is still 20/20 uncorrected, add that statement following your First-Class Medical. They expect outstanding vision in younger pilot candidates, in older applicants, it is an added bonus.

Experience

Begin with your most recent employment (civilian or military). [Include flying for the Reserves and National Guard.] State the name of your company, its location (city and state), and your dates of employment. Then give your job title and write one to three lines which describe your most important job responsibilities and achievements. (What aircraft did you fly? Where to? Passengers and/or cargo? For what purposes?) Should you choose to state your reasons for leaving the company, emphasize that it was voluntary and reflected a career growth opportunity of one kind or another in equipment advancement, scope of flying, higher position, greater responsibility, etc. Continue going back through the last ten years of your employment. Drop some of your very early nonflight-related employments, if not significant, to avoid projecting the image of being a job hopper.

If you had any changes in your job title or job assignments while with each employer and they were of an advancement nature, include them; otherwise, list only the position and salary held at the time you left.

Your chances of being considered are better if you are still employed and actively flying. If unemployed, they may wonder if you were told to leave or were fired. Avoid reference to involuntary terminations if at all possible. There may have also been personal reasons of your own which had or would have caused you to leave. Don't elaborate on the negative aspects, just the positive ones. Give the impression that each job change advanced your career in some way.

Training & Achievements

List those flight and ground schools and other programs related to your most significant ratings, certificates, and licenses, especially those considered highly reputable. State your most important flight and personal achievements— those which you think would be of interest to the airlines.

Education

This section primarily covers your formal education. The emphasis is on college. Include high school only if you had some impressive accomplishments or didn't attend college. List your degree, major field of study (minor if relevant), the university or college from which you graduated, and the year in which you graduated. State your grade average (overall and/or major) if it was B or better. Although you may have included copies of your scholarships, awards, honors, etc., in your Employment Package, also list those most significant on your Resume under this heading. If you paid for most of your college education through summer and part-time jobs, add a statement to that effect.

Personal

First list your age, height, weight, and marital status. If you are in the prime age range, simply state your age (in numbers, such as 28, 30, etc.). Should you be outside the range, use the subheading "Born," followed by your month, day, and year of birth. This makes it less readily apparent that you are younger or older than they prefer. If your height and weight are not in proportion to one another or you are extremely tall or short, you might want to leave them off of your Resume. If divorced, you might want to state "Single" or leave off marital status to avoid any negative connotations. If married, include number of children.

Then list your involvement in sports—especially those which are very competitive, both current and past, physical fitness activities (i.e. exercising, walking, jogging, running, etc.), hobbies, interests (i.e. music, photography, writing, auto mechanics, etc.), clubs and organizational memberships (community, social, and professional), both current and past. Avoid mentioning organizations which could be considered controversial because of religious, political, racial, and ethnic overtones. List any involvements you have had and offices held that indicate team effort, leadership, flexibility, diversification, and well roundedness. Don't include hunting. The reader may love animals and resent this kind of activity. Don't mention anything that the airlines might consider dangerous.

You have a good chance of hitting it off with an interviewer who has the same interests, hobbies, sports involvement, etc. It is a way to score points. Having common interests may have even played a role in the initial screening process and the decision to call you in for an interview, especially if you have devoted time to youth groups.

Many pilots include a REFERENCES heading at the bottom of their Resume, along with the statement "Available Upon Request." In essence, this conveys the message that they will provide written references if asked; otherwise they won't. A more proactive approach is recommended: Include two or three impressive letters of recommendation from prior employers in your Employment Package written by Chief Pilots or others to whom you directly report. If you don't have reference letters, provide the names, phone numbers, and addresses of your last three Chief Pilots or Commanders in an addendum to your Resume. These serve as convenient tools to begin a phone conversation for whoever is verifying your flight experience. They also serve to record another positive image of you in the minds of those who are reviewing and assessing your applicant file and background. As an added thought, you have the option of including the statement "Professional Employer Flight Reference Letters Attached" under TRAINING & ACHIEVEMENTS.

FLIGHT DATA FORM

The Flight Data Form is a supplement to your Employment Application which provides the airlines with a thorough breakdown of your flight time in each position held, type of aircraft flown, ratings, licenses, certificates acquired, etc. Be accurate, conservative, and concise in completing it and don't round off numbers on the time you have accumulated.

SUPPORTING DOCUMENTS

Supporting documents are submitted to elaborate and substantiate your technical flight qualifications and formal education. They can include:

1. Copies of your flight ratings, certificates, and licenses.
2. Letters of support from Flight Officers you know well who have been flying over six months for this airline.
3. Letters of recommendation from your last two supervisors (Chief Pilots, etc.).
4. Copies of impressive performance reviews/appraisals from two to three of your most recent supervisors. (Military pilots can submit copies of their Officer Efficiency Reports and Fitness Reports.)
5. College transcripts (if your grade average was at least C+) and a copy of your degree(s).
6. Your military release.
7. Significant honors, awards, scholarships, commendations, citations, and other special achievements.

These documents serve to substantiate what you tell the airlines in your interviews. They are also beneficial as lead information for discussion purposes when the airline is verifying your credentials. They help convince the Employment and Flight Department managers that you, indeed, have the ability to successfully complete their flight-training program and do a very effective job flying out-on-the-line.

ADDITIONAL POINTS ABOUT YOUR EMPLOYMENT PACKAGE

Female and minority Flight Officer candidates have an excellent chance of being hired by an airline which is committed to an Affirmative Action Program (AAP). If you are a female and/or minority job candidate, you might let this be known, tactfully, in your Broadcast Letter or in your Resume under PERSONAL. If you are a female and your first name could be mistaken for that of a male, state "Female" under PERSONAL. Don't make any further reference to your status beyond this point. You don't want overkill.

Samples of Resumes tailored to civilian, Naval, and Air Force Pilots, designed by the author, are provided as guides in developing your Resume. They address all the points made on effective Resume writing. You may wish to add, modify, or delete portions of the appropriate sample Resume to suit your individual needs and preferences.

Before submitting your Employment Package, have a competent writer/editor review your Cover Letter or Broadcast Letter and Resume, checking clarity, spellings, punctuation, grammar, and sentence structure. There should be no erasures or typeovers. You can seek out a seasoned secretary or manager, or anyone else in the business or education field who has strong writing and communicative skills. Your credentials should look like they were written by a professional.

To whom should you submit your Employment Package? Direct one by mail or in person (if possible) to each of the following people at the top five airlines on your airline assessment list:

1. Manager of Employment.
2. Head of the Flight Department.
3. Regional Flight Manager(s).
4. Head of the Flight Training Group.

If you have your heart set on one particular airline and that airline is currently interviewing pilots, send your first Employment Package to that airline. Then wait a reasonable period of time to hear from the airline (perhaps one to two months) before sending out a package to the next most desired airline on your list. [You don't want to get into a situation where you are contacted for an interview by your number one carrier after you have accepted a job offer and started flying with another airline which was further down your list.] It is important to direct your Employment Package to a specific person. Obtain the individual's full name and title, properly spelled, and his or her mailing address. Don't send a "Dear Sir" letter—it doesn't have a professional touch to it and will most likely be opened and read by a receptionist or secretary, not by the manager for whom it was intended. It may or may not be brought directly to his attention. The names, titles, and addresses you are seeking can be found in the World Aviation Directory, FAPA, the airline's company phone book, or obtained through a receptionist, phone operator, secretary, flight officer, or other employee working in the Personnel or Flight Department.

Some pilot candidates send their Employment Package by certified mail to have it stand out from the others. This approach has merit. Others send telegrams asking for a statement on their status. This is not recommended because it costs the airline time and money to respond to such requests, and they seldom reply. In fact, they may consider your request and technique to be in poor taste and reflective of a candidate they would not want to consider further.

Your Employment Package should be brought up-to-date and resubmitted every six months to one year. In between, you may submit item updates whenever you have a change in address, phone number(s), employers, and/or when you have significantly increased in your flight time (200 or more hours), obtained additional ratings, certificates, licenses, degrees, diplomas, and additional experience on advanced equipment, etc. Periodically revising your Employment Package helps avoid the wasted time and frustration that interviewers experience having to read through a thick applicant file, page after page, in order to piece together all of the applicant's accomplishments and assess his or her total qualifications. It is also a good idea to update your Employment Package (if needed) just prior to reporting for an interview. In fact, you may bring two or three updated Employment Packages with you and offer them to the members of the interviewing board early in the interview. This will reflect your preparedness, insight, and initiative.

STEVEN R. JOHNSON
2735 N. Taylor Street
Santa Maria, CA 93454
(805) 922-8476 (Home)
(805) 541-7948 (Message)

(Sample Civilian Male Pilot Resume)

POSITION   FLIGHT OFFICER For (Airline)

FLIGHT QUALIFICATIONS

FLIGHT TIME		RATINGS & CERTIFICATES	AIRCRAFT FLOWN
Total	2625	Flight Engineer Writtens (FEX) 95%	Fairchild Metro III
Pilot In Command ...	2341	Airline Transport Pilot—Commercial	Lear Jet 24 & 5
Turbojet	610	Single & Multi-Engine Land—Lear Jet	Cessna Citation
Turboprop	892	Flight Instructor—Certified	Beech D-18
Multi-Engine	2096	Instrument, Single & Multi-Engine	Aero Commander 680
Instrument	388	Airframe & Powerplant Mechanic	De Havilland 125
Night	991	Aircraft Dispatchers Writtens	Turbo Aztec
Cross-Country	2286	FAA First Class Medical—No Waivers	King Air F-90
Instructor	583	20/20 Vision Uncorrected—Both eyes	Piper Cheyenne

EXPERIENCE

AERO WEST, Santa Maria, California. (Month/Year) to Present
CAPTAIN on Fairchild Metroliner III for progressive commuter operating into high density airline hubs and remote airports throughout California. Approximately 75 hours flown monthly.

UNIVERSAL AIRWAYS, Miami, Florida. (Month/Year) to (Month/Year)
CAPTAIN on Lear Jet 24 & 25 with business flights throughout North, Central, and South America in all types of adverse weather. Airfields ranged from major international airports with high density traffic to small, isolated airports with limited navigational aids. Approximately 80 hours flown monthly.

PHOENIX FINANCIAL SERVICES, Phoenix, Arizona. (Month/Year) to (Month/Year)
CO-CAPTAIN on King Air F-90 flying corporate officials throughout western United States. Approximately 65 hours flown monthly.

WESTERN FLYING SERVICE, San Diego, California. (Month/Year) to (Month/Year)
FERRY PILOT/FLIGHT INSTRUCTOR. Transferred aircraft from east coast cities to Southern California on contract basis. Involved customer relations and demonstration of aircraft for retail sales. Primary, advanced, and instrument flight and ground instruction.

TRAINING & ACHIEVEMENTS

Phelps' Aeronautical Center—ATP. Accelerated Training School—FEX. Obtained FAA Ratings and PIC Status at minimum flight time. Commended for professional airmanship during airborne emergency. Founded Santa Maria Flying Club. Speak Spanish fluently. (Professional employer flight reference letters attached.)

EDUCATION

BS DEGREE in Aeronautical Operations. San Jose State University, Graduated (Month/Year). Emphasis on Maintenance Management with minor in Business Administration. Overall 3.3 grade point average. Dean's Honor Roll. Financed 90 percent college costs working part time and summers as Student Instructor, A & P Mechanic, and Reservations Agent.

PERSONAL

Age: 28; Height: 5' 11"; Weight: 165 lbs.; Marital: Married—one child
Physical Fitness: Nonsmoker, Jog, Swim, Hike, Calisthenics
Sports: Softball, Racquetball, Skiing, Tennis, Handball
Hobbies & Interests: Camping, Woodwork, Sailing, Music (Play Guitar)
Memberships: Santa Maria Flying Club, Horseless Carriage Club

1038 W. Sayre Ave.
Portland, Oregon 97229
(503) 282-7613 (Home)
(503) 292-3561 (Message)

(Sample Civilian Female Pilot Resume)

POSITION   FLIGHT OFFICER For (Airline)

FLIGHT QUALIFICATIONS

FLIGHT TIME		RATINGS & CERTIFICATES	AIRCRAFT FLOWN
Total	2705	Flight Engineer Writtens (FEX) 96%	EMB-110 Bandeirante
Pilot In Command ..	1758	Airline Transport Pilot—Commercial	DHC-6 Twin Otter
Turbojet	160	Multi-Engine Land	Cessna-402
Turboprop	794	Flight Instructor—Certified	King Air E-90
Multi-Engine	2310	Single & Multi-Engine Land	Piper Navajo PA-31
Instrument	216	Instrument Airplane	Aerostar
Night	487	FAA First Class Medical—No Waivers	Beech 99
Cross-Country	2123	20/20 Vision Uncorrected—Both eyes	Baron 58P
Instructor	914		

EXPERIENCE

SUNSET AIR, Seattle, Washington. (Month/Year) to Present
   CAPTAIN on Beechcraft Airliner (B-99) for progressive commuter operating into high density airline
   hubs and remote airports throughout Washington and Oregon. Approximately 80 hours flown
   monthly.
AIR DESTINATION, INC, Portland, Oregon. (Month/Year) to (Month/Year)
   DELIVERY PILOT. Delivered new single & multi-engine Cessna aircraft throughout western states in
   all types weather conditions. Customer relations. Approximately 70 hours flown monthly.

AERO FLIGHT CENTER, INC., Phoenix, Arizona. (Month/Year) to (Month/Year) **SENIOR FLIGHT INSTRUCTOR, ASSISTANT CHIEF PILOT, CHARTER PILOT, CORPORATE PILOT, PRIVATE & INSTRUMENT GROUND SCHOOL INSTRUCTOR.** Developed and implemented a multi-media advanced instrument ground school. Approximately 65 hours flown monthly.

DALEY COMMUNITY COLLEGE, Denver, Colorado. (Month/Year) to (Month/Year) **FLIGHT & GROUND SCHOOL INSTRUCTOR** for Department of Flight Technology. Taught private pilot ground school to career pilots. Assembled and participated in formation flying team.

TRAINING & ACHIEVEMENTS

Phelps' Aeronautical Center—ATP. Accelerated Training School—FEX. Obtained FAA Ratings and PIC Status at minimum flight time. Commended for professional airmanship during airborne emergency. Founded Oregon Flying Club. 1983 Oregon Flight Instructor Of The Year. 1985 International Organization of Women Pilot's Achievement Award. (Professional employer flight reference letters attached.)

EDUCATION

BS DEGREE in Aeronautical Studies. University of Oregon, Graduated (Month/Year). Major in Flight Technology with minor in Aviation Maintenance Technology. Overall 3.3 grade point average, Dean's Honor Roll. Financed 85 percent college costs working part time and summers as Student Instructor/Counselor, Receptionist/Cashier/Waitress.

PERSONAL

Age: 27; Height: 5' 5"; Weight: 130 lbs.; Marital: Single
Physical Fitness: Nonsmoker, Swim, Jog, Hike, Aerobics
Sports: Golf, Tennis, Volleyball, Racquetball
Hobbies & Interests: Skiing, Sailing, Horseback Riding, Guitar
Memberships: Oregon Flying Club, Aircraft Owners and Pilot Association

ANDREW K. SANDERS

1521 E. Lake Street
Oak Park, IL 60631
(312) 725-8973 (Home)
(312) 764-4311 (Message)

(Sample Air Force Pilot Resume)

POSITION FLIGHT OFFICER For (Airline)

FLIGHT QUALIFICATIONS

FLIGHT TIME		RATINGS & CERTIFICATES	AIRCRAFT FLOWN
Total	3198	Flight Engineer—Turbojet B727	C-135 (B-707)
Pilot In Command ...	2513	Airline Transport Pilot—Commercial	T-38 A/B
Jet	1685	Single & Multi-Engine Land	T-38 B
Multi-Engine	1907	Type Rated L-300	SA-226
Instrument	402	Flight Instructor—Instrument,	BE-99
Instructor	597	Single & Multi-Engine	Cessna Citation
Night	674	FAA First Class Medical—No Waivers	Light Aircraft
Cross-Country	1971	20/20 Vision Uncorrected—Both Eyes	
Instructor	266		

EXPERIENCE U.S. AIR FORCE (Month/Year) to (Month/Year)

AIRCRAFT COMMANDER—C/EC/WC-135. (Month/Year) to (Month/Year) Simultaneously qualified in all three aircraft. Commanded 16 member crew in worldwide transport of VIP/dignitaries, operating Airborne Command Post aircraft, and initial flight training to E-3A pilots. Also responsible for initial and recurring ground and flight training requirements for 75 member squadron and training of microcomputer users. Scheduled operations into busy terminal areas. Currently instruct part time.

AIRCRAFT COMMANDER—KC-135A. (Month/Year) to (Month/Year) Commanded four-member crew in aerial refueling support of multinational aircraft, transport of cargo and passengers, and airlift of critically ill personnel. Missions to Japan, Australia, South Pacific, Hawaii, Alaska, and throughout

Europe. Served as Safety Officer for two flying squadrons. Progressed to Aircraft Commander in minimum time.

COPILOT—KC-135A. (Month/Year) to (Month/Year). Assisted in the management of aircraft and air crew. Fully qualified T-38 pilot conducting cross-country proficiency flights throughout United States. Local area flights involving formation, aerobatics, and instrument procedures.

TRAINING & ACHIEVEMENTS

U.S. Air Force Training—KC-135 Combat Crew Training School—Graduated top 10 percent. Land and Water Survival Schools. Phelps' Aeronautical Center—ATP & FE. Squadron Officer School Academic Achievement Award, Oak Leaf Cluster for Meritorious Service. Air Force ROTC College Scholarship. Speak French and Spanish fluently. (Professional employer flight reference letters attached.)

EDUCATION

BS DEGREE (Cum Laude) in Aeronautical Science. Embry-Riddle Aeronautical University, Graduated (Month/Year). Overall 3.4 grade point average. Dean's Honor Roll. Course concentration on analysis of aircraft structures and design, turbojet power plants, and advanced aerodynamic theory and navigation techniques. Financed 90 percent college expenses working part time and summers as Flight Instructor, Student Teacher, Sales Clerk, and Auto Mechanic.

PERSONAL

Age: 30; Height: 6' 1"; Weight: 170 lbs.; Marital: Married—one child
Physical Fitness: Nonsmoker, Exercise Daily, Run, Swim, Hike
Sports: Handball, Golf, Tennis, Sailing, Skiing
Hobbies: Aviation Photography, Auto Mechanics, Writing, Woodwork
Interests: Aviation History, Camping, Boating
Memberships: Oak Park Flying Club, Writer's Association

JOSEPH W. MARTINEZ

1074 W. Atterberry Lane
Poway, CA 92037
(619) 743-4416 (Home)
(619) 743-3942 (Message)

POSITION   FLIGHT OFFICER For (Airline)

FLIGHT QUALIFICATIONS

FLIGHT TIME		RATINGS & CERTIFICATES	AIRCRAFT FLOWN
Total	2343	Flight Engineer—Turbojet B727	SA-3A Viking
Pilot In Command ..	1618	Airline Transport Pilot—Commercial	TA-4J Skyhawk
Jet	2014	Single & Multi-Engine Land	T-2C Buckeye
Multi-Engine	1722	ATP Type Rating—Lear Jet	T-28 B/C Trojan
Instructor	408	Instructor Pilot	PA-44-180
Instrument	346	Maintenance Check Pilot	US-3 Transport
Night	337	Special Instrument Rating	Cessna Citation
Cross-Country	1098	FAA First Class Medical—No Waivers	Piper Aztec
Simulator	240	20/20 Vision Uncorrected—Both Eyes	

EXPERIENCE   U.S. NAVY   (Month/Year) to (Month/Year)

FLIGHT OPERATIONS INSTRUCTOR. (Month/Year) to (Month/Year) Instructed in familiarization, formation, inflight refueling, and carrier qualification phases in simulators and aircraft. Designated Instrument Check Pilot, Standardization Check Pilot, Post Maintenance Check Pilot, and Flight Examiner. S-3 Carrier Operations.

AIRCRAFT COMMANDER. (Month/Year) to (Month/Year) Deployment to Western Pacific and Indian

Ocean for operations involving long range over water reconnaissance flights. Flew VIP's, passengers, and cargo between fleet units and shore stations. Collateral duties included Squadron Flight Examiner and Nuclear Weapons Training Officer. USS Enterprise.

PILOT IN COMMAND experience includes transcontinental domestic flights and all weather operations, as well as high density domestic aircraft traffic in the Southern California area.

TRAINING & ACHIEVEMENTS

U.S. Naval Air Training—Graduated top 10 percent. Accelerated Aeronautical Training—B727. Top 2 percent Officer Fitness Reports with recommendation for early promotion. Carrier Air Wing Nine Top Hook Award for Carrier Landing Proficiency. Humanitarian Service Medal. Speak Spanish conversationally. (Professional employer flight reference letters attached.)

EDUCATION

BS DEGREE in Aeronautical Systems. Purdue University, Graduated (Month/Year). Overall 3.2 grade point average. Dean's Honor Roll (College of Engineering). Course concentration on in-depth analysis of aircraft structures, turbojet power plants, aircraft design, advanced aerodynamic theory, and state-of-the-art navigation techniques. Paid 80 percent college costs working part time and summers as Student Instructor, Aircraft Fueler and Cargo Loader, Lifeguard, and Sales Clerk.

PERSONAL

Age: 30; Height: 6″ 1″; Weight: 175 lbs.; Marital: Married—2 children
Physical Fitness: Nonsmoker, Exercise Daily, Jog, Swim, Bicycle
Sports: Racquetball, Sailing, Golf, Skiing, Basketball
Hobbies: Photography, Landscaping, Building Home Furniture
Interests: History of Aviation, Camping, Boating, and Auto Mechanics
Memberships: San Diego Flying Club (organized), Toastmasters International

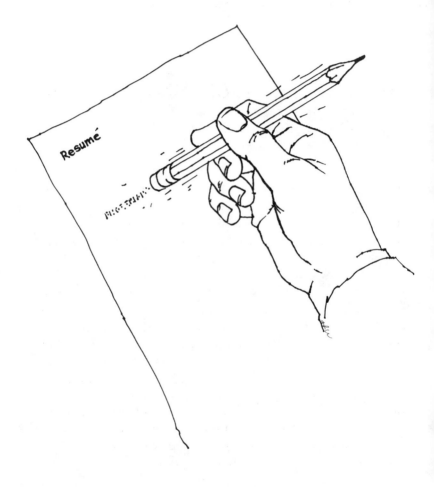

HOW TO GET PILOT INTERVIEWS

There are several direct and indirect ways, for pilot candidates to obtain interviews with the airlines. All are contingent upon the airline's applicant screening process. One method is to have your Employment Package pulled at random from the airline's job applicant files or to have it reviewed when received by mail or delivered in person. Another method involves a computerized system that identifies applicants for interview based on flight qualifications and keyed by certain cutoff levels, such as total number of flight hours, amount of multi-engine time, possession of an ATP rating or FE rating on a particular aircraft. A third path to an interview is through personal referral, recommendation, and endorsement by someone within or outside the airline who has some direct or indirect clout with senior level personnel in the Employment Department and/or Flight Department. Several airlines operate strictly on the referral/endorsement system. Others use a combination of the referral/endorsement system and the random selection system. There are a few airlines that frown upon the referral/endorsement system, and you should be cautious in approaching them. Considering, however, that the airlines often have hundreds of pilot applicants on file from which to choose every time they decide to contact people for interviews, the recommendation/endorsement referral system seems quite practical from a business "time invested versus results" perspective. It is really an indirect screening system in itself.

If you are a well-qualified candidate on paper and your applicant file is pulled for review through any system the airline uses, there is an excellent chance that you will be called in for an interview.

Under the referral system, in particular, the important point is that your file was brought to the attention of the Employment Manager or head of the Flight Department by someone who is thought to be a reputable person— someone who would use discretion and judgment in determining whom he or she would refer or recommend to the company. The pilot candidate referred will be a reflection upon this person, good or bad. In general, a greater percentage of referrals get hired than non-referrals. If you tracked 20 pilot candidates going in for interviews, 10 referrals and 10 non-referrals, you would find that more of the referrals ended up hired than the non-referrals. It pays to know someone . . . to use a myriad of network contacts.

Who are some of these personal contacts we're talking about? To begin with, receptionists have helped many pilots obtain interviews by bringing their Employment Package to the attention of the Employment Manager and adding some favorable comments. You might consider stating to her in a pleasant, personable, and sincere manner that you would greatly appreciate anything she could do to arrange an interview, and you just might succeed. If she does help to set one up for you, thank her in person, by phone, or by letter. A small token gift will also help to express your appreciation. Knowing how to present yourself impressively, in this case to the receptionist, can pay off.

There are many others within the company who could help you: stockholders, people on the Board of Directors, Regional Flight Managers, Captains, First Officers, Flight

Engineers, retired Captains and other retired employees, Flight Attendants, the airline's Flight and Ground Instructors, Flight and Crew Schedulers, Mechanics, ground crew employees, ticket and gate counter personnel, secretaries, and other personnel at all job levels and functions throughout the airline who have a good rapport with Employment and/or Flight Operations. Flying the "heavies" in a Reserve group or National Guard provides the chance to meet some airline pilots who might have excellent inside contacts. A well-worded, brief letter of support containing a request that you be interviewed from a respected Flight Officer who flies for the airline you want to join can often help to obtain interviews. It should be hand delivered to a key person in the Employment Department or Flight Operations Department who is directly involved in the process of hiring pilots. (If you are granted an interview, mention his or her name at an appropriate time during the interview.)

Accepting a position with the airlines outside of flying, in order to get your foot in the door, could enable you to establish a good performance record per se with that airline to use as a means of convincing them that you could also perform well as a Flight Officer. This approach should be considered only if your "front door" approach fails.

A technique which some pilots have used that has worked (when used very tactfully) is to personally contact a Flight Manager and say, "I would just like to meet and shake hands with you. Do you have a minute to spare?"

All these people have met you directly or through someone they know fairly well and are impressed with you— enough that they would like to see that your applicant file is pulled for review and that you have an opportunity to be called in for an interview.

There are also many personal contacts outside the company that can lead to interview appointments. These include prominent FAA officials and personnel, company clients and customers who use the airline's services, vendors who provide the airline with materiel, goods and services, people active in various community and professional clubs and organizations, church members, those in prominent government offices—city, state, or federal, sports world figures, news media writers and broadcasters, entertainment figures, college department heads, alumni, professors and placement department personnel, owners and managers of flight and ground schools, former students of yours who have good contacts, people who sell aircraft, and members of various active aviation organizations. Many of today's airline pilots can credit one or more of these contacts for opening the door to an airline interview—from that point on, they did it on their own.

Some pilots purchase one or two shares of stock in the airline they are pursuing and attend stockholders meetings where they meet influential people whose contacts can result in their obtaining an interview with the airline. Other pilots owning stock in the airline write to the President, Chairman, or Board of Directors, stating they are both a stockholder and pilot who would like to fly for their company. Of course, these approaches must be carried out very tactfully and professionally.

If you are married, your spouse can be a very valuable asset to your obtaining interviews by discreetly getting the word to possible contacts that you are seeking a Flight Officer position with the airlines and would greatly appreciate any assistance they can offer. This assistance can be in the form of contacts, suggestions, or by providing insights and answers to questions concerning the way the airline runs its hiring operation. Such additional insights could help in your receiving further employment consideration.

Relatives, friends, and neighbors can surprise you in coming up with valuable leads. They may know people who, in turn, know people who can help you.

You, yourself, may enjoy golf, tennis, bowling, skiing, racketball, handball, running or jogging and have the opportunity to make some valuable contacts through people who also enjoy the same sports and physical fitness activities. Your contact can happen at an airport terminal, restaurant, lounge, library, school, or major sport or entertainment event.

You should make a checklist of contact sources—those with whom you believe you would feel most comfortable. Then you can begin exploring all the possibilities. It is much the same as finding any job when you are out of work. If you go out every day searching, the odds are in your favor that you will find a job in a reasonable period of time. If you sit at home waiting for someone to call you, the odds of your soon getting hired are not in your favor.

You should look at getting hired from a marketing prospective. You have developed a good product, having obtained all the flight qualifications that you feel are necessary to be highly competitive for a Flight Officer position with the airlines. You have also done a good job of presenting yourself on paper through your Employment Package: you have written your advertisement for your product. Now you need to promote the product and make contacts that will lead to a sale, which is obtaining interviews with the airlines, but more important yet, actually getting hired and on board with the airline of your choice.

WHAT TO EXPECT
IN THE INTERVIEWING
AND SCREENING PROCESS

You have been successful in obtaining an interview with an airline and you have arrived for your interview appointment. What will happen to you after you step through the door of the employment office? What can you expect to happen? What is involved in the airlines's screening, interviewing, evaluation, and selection process?

There are a number of phases which you can expect to go through. How far you proceed will depend on how well you did in each prior phase of the screening. The order of these phases varies from airline to airline. For the sake of this discussion, we will conduct a walk-through of one airline's screening process.

PERSONNEL DEPARTMENT

At this particular airline, you are most likely to be interviewed first by someone from the Personnel Department: the Employment Manager, Employment Representative, or Personnel Manager. The interview can be as short as a few minutes in the case of an initial screening, or it can last for as long as an hour. It can cover a latitude of questions concerning the verification of your technical flight qualifications, education, employment record, personal data, etc. It also provides an opportunity for the interviewer to see what you look like from the perspective of the pilot image that this airline wants projected within the company, to the passengers, and to the public. You may be asked to express your ideas and opinions on a variety of topics, ranging from how you happened to choose flying as a career and why you particularly want to fly for this airline, to your personal attributes, feelings about pay systems, and career goals. Some questions might appear to be completely unrelated to a Flight Officer position. To the airlines, however, they are related in some way. How many times have you said to yourself, "Now why in the hell did they ask me that?"

FLIGHT DEPARTMENT

If, at this point in the process, you receive the Employment Department's endorsement, you will then be interviewed by the Flight Department. You can expect to talk to the Chief Pilot, a Flight Manager, or retired Captain, one at a time, or be interviewed by a panel/review board comprised of two or three of these or other Flight Management people. A First Officer and Flight Engineer may also serve as interviewers. The head of the Flight Department may want to speak with you. The Flight Managers, in many cases, are Captains who have flown the line for years and are now in a Flight Management capacity. This, in some ways, creates a crew environment (cockpit atmosphere). How well will you score with this particular crew? Occasionally a manager from another department within the airline will join the panel. Having several interviewers present at the same time has more validity than one-on-one interviews because they must reach agreement as a team. They share observations, insights, and opinions. Such a close knit team can more thoroughly discuss all aspects of your presentation and responses to their questions before reaching a group consensus on whether or not you should be hired.

Your interview with the panel may take place the same day as your interview with Employment, or it may happen the next day or a week to several weeks later. The panel interview itself may last from fifteen minutes to an hour, some shorter, some longer. The topics discussed will be similar to those covered by Employment. In addition, the panel members may look into the depth of your flight knowledge in a variety of areas that are directly related to flying, the equipment you have flown, and the conditions under which you have flown. They want to learn as much about you as they possibly can in the time allotted—help them in every way you can. Will your answers reflect the knowledge expected of you, considering your background and qualifications? The questions, and the nature in which they are asked, can often place you in a stress situation, which tests your ability to think under pressure. Will you remain relaxed or get uptight? Will you display a high degree of maturity and composure by being able to function well throughout the session?

PSYCHOLOGIST

Some airlines will also have you interviewed by a psychologist for anywhere from 15 minutes to half an hour. The questions will relate to your work experiences, educational background, personal life, family background, early childhood, strong beliefs, outside interests, career aspirations, etc. Psychologically, this is a search-and-find process to examine and assess your attitudes, viewpoints, perspectives, ideas, opinions, perceptions, insights, values, traits, motivation, and overall feeling toward yourself and others. The questions and probing boil down to this: "Are you 'put together' right? Will you fit in well with us? Will you move up the line successfully?" Candidates with strong, positive attitudes, in general, score well. Those who try hard to second guess the psychologist in their responses or clam up during the interview usually do not score well. Your goal should be to project an image of a person who is competent, confident, congenial, and always in control of any situation.

Pilot candidates, from an overall psychological perspective, can be placed into one of three bottom line categories: positive, neutral, or negative. Your goal should be to rate in the positive category. Just doing as well as other candidates will put you in the neutral group. If you are placed in the neutral or negative categories, you will probably be eliminated. The more you understand what the interviewers are looking for and are going to assess, the more prepared you can become. The more you are prepared, the calmer and more effective you will be, and the more likely you will be placed into the positive category. Do most of your in-depth thinking before the interview. You should be reviewing what areas and topics the interviewers are most likely to cover and how you plan to respond to their questions in each area. Don't wait until the interview itself to do your heavy thinking.

MEDICAL DEPARTMENT

At this point in the screening process, if you are still on "go" for continued assessment, you will be sent to take your medical examination. The airline's medical examination is much more thorough than the one administered by the FAA for a First-Class Medical. You will receive an informal but equally important interview by the physician during this examination. In most respects, it does not follow the pattern of your previous interviews since it is not firmly structured nor programmed to cover a wide range of topics and questions. In fact, it is often quite casual. Nevertheless, it is an interview and carries a significant amount of weight in the assessment process. Show that you are an alert, professional person, that you can handle stress, you care about your appearance and personal hygiene, and you are proud of your accomplishments and what you intend to accomplish. Be tactful in responding to questions asked during the physician's conversational discussions with you. This doctor represents the airline's medical perspective and critique. There are several areas of concern. The airlines prefer that you don't smoke or drink and that you go easy on sugar and caffeine. Light drinking is more acceptable than light smoking. If you have had orthokeratology or radial keratotomy treatment, you don't need to volunteer that information unless directly asked about having had such treatment. An airline physician is expected to provide the company with valuable insight into each pilot applicant from a viewpoint of projected long range health, as well as overall current health. Will you stay healthy and perform well until your retirement? You might pass the medical examination but be borderline on some of the results. You may be predisposed to a health condition which could very well present itself when you are in your forties and fifties. This condition could eventually result in a great amount of lost flying time or even a medical disability retirement. Considering this, don't volunteer significant information of a negative nature concerning the health history of your grandparents, parents, brothers, sisters, aunts and uncles such as cancer, heart problems, diabetes, hypertension, etc. It is not to your advantage to have a history of weight control problems, poor eating and sleeping habits, and drinking and smoking to excess. Don't volunteer the fact that you were adopted; an unknown family health history poses a possible future health risk. All this medical information which you have provided can influence the company's decision to hire or not hire you over another job candidate with equivalent flight qualifications.

It would be a good idea to have your own thorough medical examination long before you expect to be called in for an interview. You might be able to correct a health situation before it becomes a problem serious enough to disqualify you. It is even more important to develop a planned and controlled health program early in your life; one which will enhance your health record over the years of your flight career to the greatest extent possible.

TESTING

Many of the airlines put pilot candidates through extensive psychological, technical, and verbal testing; others do not administer written tests. The goal of most tests is to eliminate those most likely to fail in the job or field/area for which the test was designed. Cutoff scores are established. Candidates who score below the cutoff scores are generally eliminated from further consideration. Those who score above this cutoff line are thought to fit the airline's desired profile and to be those most likely to succeed—just how well they will do is not discernible. Tests must be valid (accurately predicting success on the job) and reliable (achieving consistent results when a candidate is retested).

One of the oldest known tests given in the past to airline pilot candidates is the Stanine examination. It is actually a composite of nine very comprehensive tests designed to cover all areas believed pertinent to pilot success, both flight and non-flight related, in the opinion of those who developed the tests. These tests were designed primarily to measure your flight expertise, areas of related knowledge in the science field, learning ability, potential, and psychological make-up. Airlines have shortened and modified the concepts encompassed in the Stanine to suit their particular needs. They want to determine how easily trainable you are and how well you could adapt to night flying. Many use psychological tests designed to measure how broad and well rounded you are as a person to determine how well you will adapt to others in every type of situation. Others have developed tests which cover personality traits (leadership, introversion/extroversion), values, and character; some concentrate on general knowledge. They attempt to identify loner-type of people and those with negative attitudes. You can also expect to be tested on color differentiation, mathematics, physics, mechanics, letter and number stress, perception, motor abilities, etc. Brush up on regulations, your knowledge of mechanics, electrical applications, and physics in particular before going in to take your tests.

Most of the airlines will also put you through a flight simulator test on their equipment or whatever simulator is available. You will be asked to perform a number of flight maneuvers e.g., takeoffs, climbs, turns, banks, descents, holding, tracking, ILS approaches) on heavy jet equipment. You will probably be given one or two problem conditions with which to cope. You most likely will deal with five basic instruments. Distractions may be purposely programmed to test your basic flying skills and your ability to handle unexpected situations. The fact that you have never had the opportunity to fly this particular equipment, plus your lack of familiarization with it, is taken into consideration. Don't hesitate to pursue assertively your altitude, air speed, and heading throughout the check ride. You would find it beneficial to practice in a flight simulator, go back over your basic instrument fundamentals and training, and review your planning procedures beforehand. Your adaptability, behavior, and reactions throughout the simulator test are closely monitored. It is the airline's best opportunity to observe you under stress and to note some of your thresholds of tolerance to pressure while in action. Remember that when you are seated in the simulator, you become the Captain. Keep your aircraft in trim. Approach the entire simulator check as the Captain, displaying the self-confidence of a Captain in charge of the aircraft.

In the past, some airlines used polygraph testing. There is really not much that can be done to improve polygraph scores—just play it straight and be honest. It was used to uncover hidden criminal convictions, significant drug use or involvements, falsification of flight qualifications, and similar pertinent information.

You should be aware that there may be deliberate distractions that are programmed to occur while you are being tested. This is intended to determine how easily you are distracted and if you can handle the stress created by such distractions. Show that you can concentrate on the test materials and instructions while, at the same time, you are aware of the distractions and could identify them if requested to do so. [Some carriers want to measure your total awareness at all times.]

According to research studies there are several ways for you to raise your test scores. You should get a good night's sleep two nights before you are to take your battery of tests. Eat nourishing meals. Breathe lots of fresh air. Do not cram for your tests. Practice taking tests. If you have the opportunity to be tested at a college, business, industrial, or governmental employment placement or counseling office, do so. The studies also indicate that if you complete reading courses, expand your areas of reading materials, and increase your vocabulary you will do better on tests. You might want to consider applying for some positions at companies that are in an aviation-related field where testing is a part of the applicant screening process—just for the opportunity to practice taking tests. The same thinking can also be applied to being interviewed: practice with good insight for improvement increases your chances of getting hired—you become a more proficient applicant. Note that the interview itself is really an essay test. You are not restricted to true or false replies or multiple choice answers. You have an open-ended opportunity to succeed or fail. In general, pilots come closer to one another in test scores but are much farther apart on interview results.

The tests that airlines administer to their Flight Officer candidates usually have material coverage similar to one another, with the same ultimate purpose in mind: accurately predicting pilot success, out on the line, flying for their company. Each has a profile that reflects the ingredients of success for their particular airline. They look for pilot candidates who come as close as possible to matching this profile.

BACKGROUND INVESTIGATION

Most airlines conduct a background investigation to verify your educational accomplishments, degrees, grades, employment history (including dates of employment), positions held, your job responsibilities and overall performance (if the company you were with is willing to release that information). Airlines also want to verify your flight ratings and licenses, and any other area of concern that might have surfaced during your interview. You should have the information available as to who they can check with to verify what you have told them with reference to your prior experience (names, addresses, and phone numbers of your last three supervisors, etc.). Let them also know, if possible, who they should contact to verify your college degree and other formal educational accomplishments. Mix-ups can be costly and have happened. If you provide this information, it can speed up your background investigation and possibly make the difference between being selected for an earlier or later class or even being selected at all. If the airlines can't contact key people to check you out, you are not likely to get hired. There has to be positive reinforcement and verification of your technical flight qualifications and the level of your performance as a pilot.

RETURN ON INVESTMENT

You must remember that airlines are essentially profit-making organizations and are concerned primarily with "return on investment." For every dollar they spend on pilot recruitment, salaries, benefits, training and recurrent training, there must be more than a dollar return earned through actual hours flown by those same pilots over their years of employment with that airline. The more hours flown and the higher the position attained (preferably upgrading to Captain as quickly as possible), the greater the return on investment.

"Which do you love most: dogs or cats?"

"Let's give it another try."

CHAPTER 8

HOW TO DRESS APPROPRIATELY FOR AN INTERVIEW

Airlines often hire in their own image. The dress and appearance of airline personnel are very important to this image. Your prospects of being hired are considerably enhanced by the proper clothes and your overall, personal appearance during your interviews. This chapter highlights some of the things you should consider as you prepare to present yourself in the best light possible.

MEN

SUITS

You should wear a new tailored suit of good quality . . . single-breasted and dark, solid blue, brown, or gray (no blazers or sweaters). If you want to appear younger or heavier, select a lighter shade of one of these basic colors. A dark suit tends to take off pounds and add a few years; a lighter suit can add pounds and take off a few years. Plaid suits or those with pronounced design are not recommended. Don't wear an old suit that still looks new, but is out of style. Allow a half-inch of shirt cuff to show on the coat sleeves and the same amount of shirt collar to show around the back of the neck. The collar and lapels should hug your neck and body and not creep-up when you bend over. Your pants legs should hang straight without breaking, down to the top of your shoes.

It's a good idea to dress as though you were going to your interview and then visit one or two clothing stores that carry a better line of men's suits. Ask a seasoned salesperson if he or she feels that you are appropriately dressed for the kind of interview you have in mind and if there are any suggestions for improving your professional image. Most of these people will give you an honest opinion. They may suggest a change in an accessory item, but seldom will they pressure you into buying a new suit. Your rule of thumb should be to dress well enough to be mistaken for a professional business manager.

When you travel to your interview, you should bring along an additional suit in case you are asked to return the next day for further screening or in the event your original suit is accidentally soiled and you haven't time to take it to the cleaners. Don't wear your suit on the flight; save it for the interview.

At the interview, don't take off your suit coat unless you are asked to do so. You are expected to maintain a high level of professionalism and decorum.

SHIRTS

You should wear a long-sleeve, solid white or very light-color shirt that matches your suit color and has a standard collar. Don't wear a patterned shirt. A shirt that has never been worn is better than one that has been laundered.

TIES

It is professional to wear a new tie the same color as your suit or one mainly solid with a few narrow stripes in colors that reflect different tones of the suit. The style should be up-to-date in its width and knot (leaning toward a half-Windsor knot). It is best to not wear a collar pin, stickpin, tie clip, lapel pin, cuff links, or bracelet. These and other accessories could appear gaudy or in poor taste.

SHOES

Appropriate dress shoes have medium heels and are brown (to match a brown or beige suit), black (to match a blue or gray suit), or camel (to match other suit colors). Choose conservative, wingtip or plain-looking slip-on shoes that don't have a pronounced buckle or decorative feature.

SOCKS

Your socks should be new and in a solid color which is as close as possible to the color of your suit. They should be calf length and should fit snugly; they should never tend to slip down.

BELTS

A new leather belt the color of your shoes or suit looks very professional. The belt buckle should be small or moderate and traditional in style. Large, ornate belt buckles are not professional.

RINGS

If you are married, you should wear your wedding ring. Wearing additional rings is not recommended.

HAIR

Your hair should be moderate in length, cut slightly above the top of your ears. The style should be traditional/conservative . . . no new looks. Your hair should be cut or trimmed about three days before your interview.

Moustaches should be kept trim and short. You may encounter an interviewer who does not like moustaches but will accept them if they are neat and trim rather than bushy. If you don't want to chance the risk of meeting an interviewer who frowns on moustaches, shave yours off. Beards are not acceptable to the airlines.

If your hair loss is significantly noticeable, it would be acceptable to wear a well-made hair piece that fits well and looks natural in color and style. If your hair is graying and you wish to appear younger, you may want to use a coloring agent that matches your natural hair color.

BRIEFCASE

You should carry a quality, plain-looking, new briefcase to the interviews. It should contain your log books, resumes, college transcripts, letters of recommendation and commendation, copies of ratings, certificates, licenses, degrees, and other supporting documents that you might be asked to show or that you will want to refer to during the interviews.

WOMEN

SUITS

To project a professional image, you should wear a quality, solid-color suit with tailored skirt in navy blue, dark brown, camel, or charcoal gray. No vest. A plaid suit is acceptable if the patterns are not pronounced and the suit appears to be a solid color. The material should be wool, linen, cotton, or synthetics that look like these materials. The color should compliment your skin tone. Plan to take two skirt suits (not of the same color) in the event you are asked to return the next day for additional interviews. It is advisable to purchase your ensemble at a better women's apparel store that has an excellent reputation and a seasoned sales staff. Inform the salesperson that you are dressing for an important interview and you want to appear professional, feminine, and conservative. You will probably be given several options that satisfy your purpose and taste. The suit you choose should fit comfortably. The collar should cling to the contour of your neck and show a half-inch of your blouse. The collar and lapels should lie flat and roll with the jacket. The sleeve length should allow a half-inch of the blouse cuff to show. The skirt should fall just below the knees.

BLOUSE

You should wear a tailored, solid white, long-sleeve blouse without frills. Both the cut and buttons should be simple. Choose solid cotton or silk or a synthetic that projects the same appearance but doesn't cling to you or shine. Leave the top button open or wear it buttoned with an ascot-style woman's necktie or scarf that complements your jacket in style and color.

SHOES

Wear quality, low-heel, plain, dark-color pumps to match your skirt suit. You will need an extra pair of shoes to wear that will match the color of your second suit.

HOSE

Skin-color pantyhose should be worn.

COAT

If the weather requires a coat, it should be a wraparound wool cloth coat with a plain collar. The length should cover the bottom of your suit skirt. It should have a cloth belt, few pockets, and no gaudy buttons.

GLOVES

Wear dark-color, close fitting, leather gloves in winter.

HAIR

You should select a well-respected hair stylist to style your hair. Inform her/him that you want to look stylish, conservative, and feminine (but not sexy) at an important interview for a professional position. Your hair should be moderate in length, shoulder length at most. You don't want to look boyish or masculine or to have excessively curly or wavy hair. If your hair is prematurely graying, it's acceptable to dye it the same color as your natural hair. Have your hair cut and set a day or two before your interview.

MAKEUP

You should wear little or no makeup except for possibly a little lipstick. Keep your eyebrows natural-looking; darken them slightly if necessary to accentuate them. A very limited amount of eye shadow or eye liner can be used (in good taste) if you feel it enhances your appearance.

NAILS

Your fingernails should be kept short to moderate in length, never long. The nail polish used should be colorless. Artificial nails are not recommended.

PERFUME

Use very little or no perfume. A slight scent of light-smelling cologne is acceptable.

JEWELRY

Wear a minimum amount of very simple jewelry . . . perhaps some plain gold or silver posts if your ears are pierced, a tastefully designed watch and band, and a small ring that lies relatively flat on your finger.

HANDBAG

You should not bring a handbag to the interview. It will restrict your hand movements and gestures during the interview or have to be placed on the floor or on a desk or nearby table.

ATTACHE CASE

Carry your flight credentials and supporting documents and papers to the interview in a slim, dark-color, quality leather case or one with the appearance of leather.

WHAT PAPERWORK
TO BRING WITH YOU

To be well prepared for your interview, you should bring your log books, copies of your ratings, certificates, licenses, degree, birth certificate, social security card, military release, extra copies of your Resume (to offer to someone on the interviewing panel who is sharing your Resume with another panel member), college transcript, and impressive letters of recommendation from your last two or three supervisors (if you didn't include these in your Employment Package). You will usually be told what documents you must bring and when to bring them; the others are brought just in case they are also asked for. Don't give away your original documents—just copies. You will appear more professional if these documents are carried in a briefcase or attaché case (yours or borrowed from a friend).

Reference letters from your previous supervisors are useful to the interviewer(s) or investigators for making phone or written contacts with past employers to verify your employment and performance record. Letters of recommendation from peers and others with good reputations who know your flight performance record well are also advantageous, but these carry less weight. References from people who know you personally, but not as a pilot, carry the least weight—the exception being those from prominent figures well known to airline personnel.

If you are questioned on your log books, you should answer briefly and to the point. Your unsolicited comments could be misinterpreted as an attempt to cover up something questionable. You should not have any flight time in your log books that cannot be verified.

"Now, where did I put that envelope?"

CHAPTER 10

CREATING A FAVORABLE
FIRST IMPRESSION

At this point you have done all the right things to obtain your interview, to prepare your materials and yourself, and to get your act together. Now, it's time for your interview. It's an important moment, which may determine the whole course of your future career. Naturally, you are both excited and apprehensive. The author of this book understands how you feel, having spent ten years as Manager of Employment for a major international airline and having been responsible for the screening, assessment, and selection of pilot candidates.

The interviewing and assessment process is complex and comprehensive. A great deal happens, some of which is visible and apparent to you, and much of which is invisible and not readily apparent. You hear questions and give answers, but you don't know what the interviewers are thinking as they listen to your responses. You're really not certain whether you are scoring or losing points.

There are many things that airline interviewers look for, weigh and measure, from the moment you enter their offices until you leave. These factors are consciously and subconsciously being considered. The interviewers like some candidates, and they don't like other candidates. Why? They themselves don't always know why. They have a good feeling about certain candidates, whom they would like to see hired. On the other hand, they just cannot envision certain candidates developing into future successful Captains with their airline. What causes them to feel this way? How are favorable and unfavorable impressions created? The answers to these questions are the guts of this book.

When does your image building begin? It starts with your arrival for your interview and is the first of many impressions you will make on those with whom you come in contact. Make it a positive impression. Arrive fifteen minutes to half-an-hour early. There are reasons why this could work to your advantage. A problem situation could have arisen unexpectedly, earlier that day, and one of the interviewing panel members has to catch a flight that afternoon. The interviewing board is hoping you will arrive early. If you do, it will enable them to begin their interview with you much earlier than scheduled and allow enough time for that one board member to make his or her flight. Perhaps the panel has wrapped-up a prior interview earlier than expected and are ready to begin yours. If you don't take the initiative to arrive early in anticipation of such circumstances, your whole interview could be off to a shaky start.

The first person you are likely to meet is the receptionist. Approach her in a very tactful manner and ask if she might possibly have the time to provide the names, spelling, pronunciation, and titles of the interviewers. You don't want to butcher the way in which you address them during introductions nor during the course of your interview. This information also will help you to accurately address "Thank You" letters, which you should send to each of the interviewers after you return home. It is the professional way to go!

While you are waiting in the lobby, try to relax! Unbutton your suit coat. (Button it again when you spot the interviewer headed your way.) Read something light. It will help to ease the tension and allow you to perform better during the interview. You should have done all your interview preparation "homework" by now. If you need to use the restroom, this is the time to do so. Avoid getting so involved in a conversation with another applicant that you don't notice the interviewer approaching you. The interviewer should not have to get your attention. You should be waiting alertly for him or her to arrive.

From the very first meeting, support personnel such as secretaries, receptionists, nurses, people involved in testing, etc., can and will volunteer favorable or unfavorable comments about you to the interviewers. These comments can add to or subtract from the points earned on your image score. Here are some typical comments: "You're going to hire . . . (pilot candidate) aren't you? He's/She's very nice! Mixes well with the other candidates." Or, "You're not going to hire . . . (pilot candidate) are you? He's/She's not too personable. Seems a little pushy." You should consider some sincere compliments to these people about their voice, smile, personality, professionalism, brisk work pace, or some other real attribute [no B.S.]. This minor form of flattery can go a long way when done in good taste.

How do you create that very important "good first impression?" When the interviewer approaches you and introduces himself or herself, rise in a brisk but smooth manner, look straight into his or her eyes, smile, present a firm handshake, and say, "It's a pleasure to meet you, Captain/Mr./Ms./Mrs./Miss . . . !" (When you don't smile, you may appear to be unfriendly, tense, uptight, or frightened.) The interviewer should never have to stand with his or her hand out, waiting for you to get up and shake hands. If the interviewer does not introduce himself or herself and remains silent to see what you will do in such a situation, it is then acceptable to introduce yourself. This can display tactful initiative on your part, under stress. Show from the very beginning of your initial meeting that you are pleasant, polite, relaxed, enthusiastic, and alert—a person who immediately projects a positive image. Throughout the interview ahead, continue to convey that same impressive image. Don't be afraid to show that you're also a warm and sincere person. Smile from time to time and look pleasant. Show pride in your past performance and accomplishments, and a self-confidence that is tempered with humility. Does all of this sound too "put on." Experience in the real world has proved that if you can do it smoothly and make it seem natural, you will earn more points in the scoring.

When you accompany the interviewer to the interviewing office, never drop behind more than half a step, making it difficult for him or her to carry on a brief conversation with you while walking. The interviewer should not have to slow down for you.

After you enter the interviewing office, stand and wait until you are asked to be seated. Don't immediately sit down in the first chair you see—it might be the interviewer's chair! You should sit down as the interviewer sits down. If it's a Board Interview, sit down at the same time the last Board Member sits down.

CHAPTER 11

SPEAKING THE RIGHT "BODY LANGUAGE"

Body positioning, posture, and movements communicate a non-verbal language that interviewers understand, consciously or subconsciously. This "body language" conveys images of you as clearly as the words you use throughout your interview. Your body can say, "I'm an open, relaxed professional person," or "I'm a tense, guarded, and cautious person."

Your first positive image is conveyed by sitting erect, with your butt all the way to the back of the chair and your shoulders flat against the back. Don't sit at the edge or middle of the chair. If you are a man, sit with your legs apart—about the width of the chair legs, and your feet flat on the floor. When you want to release some pent-up energy during the interview, shift your legs so that your right ankle crosses your left knee. Do your repositioning after you have answered a question and the interviewer is looking down at your Employment Application—not while you are talking and he or she is closely observing you. If you are a woman, you can sit with your legs crossed at the knees or with your ankles crossed. Also, do not shift positions while you are talking or being closely observed. Your fingers should be slightly coupled, with your left hand resting on your left leg and your right hand resting on your right leg. Don't fold your arms, clasp your hands tightly together, hold your hands up toward your face while talking, or touch the desk or table in front of you. If you wish, you can bring the tips of your fingers together or place the fingers of your left hand loosely around your right wrist. You must never point with your finger to information on your Resume or Employment Application in responding to an interviewer's question. It would appear as though you were saying, "Look Dummy, it's right there—can't you read?" If the chair offered to you is quite far away from the desk or table that you are facing or if the chair does not directly face the interviewer(s), take the initiative to straighten it and move it closer in.

As to body movement, it's advantageous to gesture and show enthusiasm but don't go overboard—no sweeping hand or arm movements. Express your sincerity not only through finger and hand movements but in your facial expressions as well. Smile often, move your head once in a while, and speak with your eyes! Loosen up! A tense, immobile body with little or no facial expression conveys a cold, insensitive image.

Interviewers also look for signs of stress to questions asked by watching to see if you change your behavior—scratch your nose, blink several times, clear your throat, frequently shift in your chair while talking, raise or lower your voice, talk faster or slower, or look away and break eye contact. These are all indications that you have become uncomfortable and they alert the interviewer to dig further into the question(s) being asked at the time your behavior changed.

You should pay attention to the body language of the interviewers. Are you holding their attention? If so, you are on target. If they begin to "shift gears" (in any area), it means they want to move on to another question. Some will shuffle your paperwork, pick up or lay down their pen, or look away from you. When you observe this happening, it's time to wrap up your answer.

Your eye contact with the interviewer is very important. You should maintain eye-to-eye contact approximately 80 percent of the time; especially while you are being asked a question, gathering your thoughts, beginning your answer, and wrapping up the tail-end of your reply. The 20 percent of the time when you are looking away during your reply is intended to give both the interviewer and yourself a break. Look away diagonally upward to the left or right of the interviewer. Don't drop your head and look downward—which has a negative connotation. Constant eye contact can make most interviewers uncomfortable. When being interviewed by a panel/board, divide your eye contact equally among all the members. Resist the tendency to concentrate your attention on the person who seems most receptive, who smiles, nods frequently as though in agreement, and gives you undivided attention. If you direct your gaze too much to any one person, the others will feel ignored and be more critical in their scoring.

The silent message...

OPENING THE INTERVIEW

The first objective on the list of most interviewers is to put you at ease, establish a rapport with you, and "open you up." They do this with light conversation which is usually unrelated to your qualifications, such as your flight to their location, the weather, a current event/news story, a mutual acquaintance, etc. You should join in this conversation in a positive way. Don't give a three-word response. The interviewers are trying to perceive how easy it might be for other pilots and passengers to generate a pleasant conversation with you. (Note: after a few minutes into the interview, nonchalantly unbutton your suit coat again—you have made a good initial impression, now make yourself more comfortable.)

You should not initiate the interview—this is the interviewer's prerogative. Don't address the interviewer by his or her first name unless you're asked to do so. Many people strongly resent a person who is a total stranger assuming personal familiarity until that familiarity is mutually established. Follow the interviewer's lead—don't lead the way. As the conversation proceeds, you may vary the manner in which you address the interviewer. At times it could be "Well, Captain Jones" or Captain . . ." or "Sir . . ." or "Mr./

Ms./Mrs./Miss Jones." At other times you should answer the question directly without formally addressing the interviewer.

When you know what you are talking about, give your answer with full conviction, then remain silent so the interviewer can comment on your answer or ask a follow-up question. If, however, you are not certain, be humble and reply, "To the extent that I have had some exposure to that equipment, I would say . . . ." If you do not know the answer to the question, say so . . . "I really cannot answer that question. I don't have the experience, education, training, or ratings required in that area to give you a meaningful answer. I would only be guessing." Interviewers sometimes ask questions they know you are not qualified to answer in order to determine if you are the type of person who tries to bluff his or her way through interviews.

You need to get a feel for the interviewer and adjust your approach accordingly. Observe closely whether the interviewer presents a light or serious mood, is relaxed or uptight, is quiet or talkative, seems to be in a hurry or has a lot of time, etc. By following the interviewer's lead, you can proceed more smoothly through the interview while still maintaining a strong professional image. You must treat all interviewers equal, whether male or female and regardless of level of position, age, race, nationality, or other distinguishing characteristics. Any special treatment (buttering up) on your part will be readily apparent.

It is always good form to thank the interviewer for the opportunity to meet him or her and to be interviewed. You might do this just before you are asked your first important question or just at the close of the interview.

At the beginning and throughout the interview, the interviewer (or panel of interviewers) will ask a lot of questions on many different subjects. You are expected to give logical, clear, candid replies, with occasional comments on the subject; however, you must not attempt to control or dominate the interview at any time. Whenever you have the opportunity, of course, you may acceptably take the initiative and add any related aviation knowledge that you may have gained from you avocations, hobbies, reading, etc., to reinforce your qualifications.

CHAPTER 13

WHAT YOU'RE REALLY TELLING THEM

Let's talk about the heart of any interview between two or more persons. What's really happening? Every time you say anything to an interviewer, you are in essence communicating in three ways:

1. You are conveying *information* (content)—in answer to a question asked or in making a comment. Is this information accurate, applicable, and important?

2. You are conveying your *attitude*—toward the information which you are presenting to the interviewer through the tone of your voice, your loudness or softness, your speed of delivery, your choice of words, your length of reply, and your overall conciseness or vagueness. Is this attitude positive, neutral, or negative?

3. You are conveying *body language*—through your posture, what you do with your hands, arms, legs and feet, the tenseness in your facial expressions, your gestures, body movements, and frequent change in body movements. Is this body language appropriate to the occasion and favorable to you?

What do these methods of communicating all mean to the interviewer? They either confirm or deny the information that you are relating in answering questions or responding to comments. Are you believable? All three may support one another or one may deny the truthfulness of the other two. Are all three of your communication techniques in sync? In particular, when you are explaining any negative event or incident you have experienced, don't lose control of your emotions and begin expressing any deep bitterness through your voice, words, or body movements.

"Hire me!"

A BRIEF RESPITE

And some thoughts for conjecture . . .

"A pilot has an office with three windows and the greatest view in the world."

"Know how to take aim at what you want and when it's time to pull the trigger."

"Don't mistake activity for achievement."

"If you are a wise pilot, you assume you can never know all there is to know about flying."

"Stress occurs when you won't accept the possibility of failure."

"If you don't manage your mind, it will manage you."

"The first step to success is visualizing it."

"Beliefs are the creative source of reality."

"There are no problems—only problem makers."

CHAPTER 14

PACING YOURSELF
DURING THE INTERVIEW

Some of the questions asked in interviews simply call for an answer of three or four words—others may require a reply of four or five sentences. In general, your replies should vary in length from very short and to-the-point answers to more elaborate answers—in proportion to the depth, breadth, seriousness, and complexity of the subject. If you were asked, for example, about your overall grade average in college, you would be expected to give a brief reply. If, however, you were asked why you chose to major in a particular field in college, it could take several sentences to give a full explanation.

The timing of your answers is important. At certain times, you are expected to respond to a question immediately without hesitation. At other times, you are expected to pause, think in silence for a few seconds, then give your answer. You don't want to start talking until you know exactly what you are going to say; otherwise, you appear impulsive and not well organized. Don't give the impression that you are playing the whole interview by ear, saying whatever pops into your mind at the time.

Some questions pose a problem situation and can be best answered by presenting several options or alternative answers, along with the reasons why you considered each alternative, then boiling it down to that alternative which, in your opinion, would offer the best solution. Role playing situation questions are usually answered in this matter.

The intent behind a question asked may not be readily apparent. At times, interviewers ask leading questions and don't expect you to be "sucked in" by them. At other times, questions or statements are presented in a manner that suggests you would probably agree with them, but in essence, they really hope that you won't go along with them because the statement isn't true or there are other factors to be considered. Ask yourself, "Why are they asking me this?" Understanding why will give you more insight into answering the question to their satisfaction.

Gear yourself to the pace set by the interviewers. If they seem to want to move along rather quickly or slow down the pace, follow their lead. It indicates your insight and ability to adjust quickly to any changing condition—this is most important to effective team interaction.

CHAPTER 15

QUESTIONS ASKED
IN INTERVIEWS

This chapter covers typical questions that are asked by the interviewers of pilot candidates. These questions represent a composite of those asked by regional, national, and international airlines as well as commuter airlines. Some airlines revise their questions periodically, and some gear their questions to the specific background of the pilot candidate. In some cases, they are the same questions worded differently. Each airline has certain questions that pertain to its primary areas of concern. All of the questions, however, call for more than "yes" and "no" answers. You might even be asked two or three questions in rapid order to determine how quickly and effectively you react under pressure. Could you answer each one, in the order given, to the depth and extent expected of a strong candidate?

You are better off preparing many good answers in advance, almost to the point of overkill, because you are bound to forget some answers through interview nervousness and will come up short if you don't compensate accordingly.

The following questions are categorized under prime areas of coverage for your convenience in referring back to those that you should spend more time on to develop better answers.

ESTABLISHING INITIAL RAPPORT

- How long have you been waiting out there?
- Is it still raining outside?
- Is this the first time you have been to our area? Did you have a difficult time finding our office?
- How do you pronounce your last name?
- Do you go by your full first name? What do most people call you?
- How was your trip out here?
- Wasn't that something about . . . (comment on a significant current event occurring within or outside aviation).
- I see you know . . . (name of employee). How well do you know him/her?
- Tell me about yourself.
- What have you been doing lately?
- What would you like to talk about?

OTHER AIRLINES

- Which airlines have you applied with? Why did you choose those in particular? Why haven't you applied with other carriers? Which three airlines would you most want to fly for? For what reasons?
- Have you had any interviews? With whom? What was the outcome of each? Why weren't you hired?
- Do you have any job offers pending? With whom?
- If you received a job offer from another airline while we were still considering you, what would you do?
- How would you differentiate an average airline from an exceptional one?
- What would you look for in an airline as a pilot? As a passenger?
- What problems do the airlines face today?

THIS AIRLINE

- Why do you want to fly for us? What attracts you to our airline? What do we have going for us over other carriers? Anything else?
- What do you want out of us?
- What can we expect to get out of you?
- Will our company be asking for productivity increases from our pilots?
- Why did you wait so long to apply with us?
- Have you applied with us before and been turned down? When?
- Tell us in one or two words why you're here?
- How much do you know about us? Where did you learn this? What is the history of our company?
- Where are our headquarters, training center, and maintenance base located?
- Who is our CEO? President? Head of our Flight Department? Who was our last CEO?
- Who is the most important person in the company? Why?
- How many pilots do we have? How many total employees?
- What do we pay Flight Engineers during their first year with us?
- How much do you know about our training program?
- What is the size and composition of our fleet? How many . . . (name of specific aircraft) do we have? How many on order? How much do you know about our new . . . (aircraft)? What are the advantages and disadvantages of a . . . (aircraft) over a . . . (aircraft)?
- What is our route structure? Are you aware of our recent expansion plans? Our pending merger/ takeover?
- How has our profit picture looked this past year?
- What is our stock currently selling for? Do you own any of our stock?
- What are our annual revenues?

- Where are our domiciles?
- What union represents our pilots?
- How long is the probationary period for new Flight Engineers?
- What do you think is our biggest problem?
- Do you know anyone who works for us? Who? Where? Doing what? How long?

GETTING INTERESTED AND STARTED IN FLYING

- When did you first get interested in flying? How old were you? How did it happen?
- When did you decide you were going to be a pilot?
- When did you start developing a career plan to acquire your flight credentials?
- How and when did you actually get started in flying? Where did you begin flying? Why did you wait so long?

WHY BE A PILOT

- Why did you decide to become a pilot? Why not some other career?
- What is there about flying as a career which appeals to you more than any other profession?
- What do you enjoy most about flying? Least?
- Why do you want to be an airline pilot?
- If you weren't a pilot, what would you be? Why?

CAREER GOALS AND PROGRESSION

- What are your career goals?
- What has been the apex of your career so far?

- What did you do to help upgrade yourself in all your jobs?
- Would you rather be a pilot or flight instructor? Why?
- Would you be interested in a management position we have open? Why? Why not?
- What would be your fantasy job if you could be anyone you wanted to be or could have any job you wanted to have?
- If you were to receive two job offers, both from the airlines, at the same time, which would you choose and why?
- What makes a professional pilot?
- Why do you want to be a Captain?
- How long do you think it will take to advance to a Captain's seat in our company? When do you feel you would be ready to move up to that position?
- Considering all your PIC time, why would you be interested in a Second Officer's position? Won't you be frustrated having to work yourself back up again? Would you be satisfied being a Flight Engineer for ten years?
- If, for medical reasons, you could no longer fly, what would you do?
- Would you rather be a First Officer on a 747 or Captain on a 727?
- Would you rather fly passengers or freight? Why? Domestic or international? Why?
- Outside of flying, what other jobs could you perform for us?
- Why did you get out of aviation for . . . (period of time/another field)?

TECHNICAL QUALIFICATIONS AND TRAINING

- How much do you know about our training program? How did you learn of this?

- How old were you when you received your Private License. At what age did you solo?
- Which of your ratings, license, and certificates do you think are most important? Why?
- Where did you receive your ratings? When? What impressed you the most about the flight training you have received? Least? Describe the quality of that training.
- Did you complete every training program which you began? Why not?
- How important do you feel an ATP and FE rating are to an airline? What score did you make on your FE Writtens? ATP? Why so low? How did you study for them?
- How did you finance for your training? How much did you yourself contribute?
- What was your standing in class for each training program you completed?
- Having been a flight instructor, what are the different styles of teaching? Which do you favor? Why? What characteristics would make it difficult for a person to learn to fly?
- What is the maximum landing weight of a . . . (aircraft)? How much runway do you need?
- Does it take longer to get off the ground on a moist or dry day (relative humidity)?
- If given only three basic instruments to fly an aircraft, which would you choose?
- What is the freezing level (altitude reached) when the ground temperature is known?
- Did you ever fail an annual checkout? When? Where? Why?
- Why haven't you stayed current?
- Why should we hire you over someone who has more training, ratings, and hours?
- Questions on wind shear, compass systems, elevations of lakes and airfields, instruments, control systems, power plants, electrical, mechanical, and hydraulic systems, humidity, clouds, icing, snow, fog, and other

weather conditions, load factors, temperature limitations, idle fuel flow, and aircraft fuel capacities—all have been asked individually or, at times, in conjunction with role playing in a simulated situation. Problem cases are presented involving some of these and you are asked how you would handle them.

OVERALL QUALIFICATIONS

- If you were hiring pilots, what qualifications would you look for? In what order of importance? Why? What questions would you ask? What do you think we are looking for? Which do you think are most important to us? Why? What qualities are most important to you?
- What prompted you to select the particular direction you have gone in acquiring your flight credentials?
- What are the negatives you have experienced in your career?
- Would you share your thoughts with us on "complacency," as it relates to our type of business.
- Have you ever had any trouble being a woman in this business?
- Would it bother you being away from home so much?
- How good a pilot are you?
- What makes a good pilot? Bad pilot? What kind of pilot are you?
- What can you do to further increase your qualifications? Any plans? What are they?

PILOT JOB RESPONSIBILITIES?

- What are the most important aspects of a pilot's job?
- In what ways can a pilot interact effectively with other crew members?

- Which do you think is most important—individual or team performance? Why?
- What are the most important job responsibilities of a Flight Engineer, First Officer, and Captain? What are all the various roles a Captain plays? What can you do as an FE or First Officer to make the Captain's performance more successful?
- What types of teaching have you done? In your opinion, do you learn more receiving instruction or giving it? What are the advantages and disadvantages of being a flight instructor? How many students have you instructed? Who was your first student? How would you handle a difficult student? What was it that made him/her difficult to instruct?
- How would you "keep current" while a Flight Engineer? How would you feel about being "on reserve"? What are the benefits of being a Flight Engineer?
- What does "crew concept" mean to you?
- What were the most important job responsibilities you have ever held?
- How would you react in an airborne emergency?
- What would you do if you lost your compass on an approach?
- What is the most dangerous aspect of flying?
- What type of flying do you enjoy most?
- Have you ever flown with a Captain who you thought was dangerous?
- Would you turn in another pilot if he broke an FAR? If your Captain wasted fuel?
- When did you have to correct a Captain or co-pilot? What was his/her reactions?
- If your Captain performed a maneuver which you questioned, what would you do? Would you speak up?

FLIGHT EXPERIENCE

- How did you obtain your flying jobs?

- Which of all your jobs did you enjoy most? Least? How did you benefit from each job held?
- Do you do any other flying outside your present job/ company? Where? What type?
- How do you feel, in general, about your job and salary progression?
- Who were the best and worst Captains you have known? How would you describe an impressive Captain? What differentiates an outstanding Captain from a good one?
- Have you ever had a conflict with a Captain? How did you handle it?
- What did you think of the supervision you received in your last three jobs? How would you describe your working relationship with each supervisor? Who did you enjoy working for the most? Least? If we phoned your last boss and asked him or her about you, what do you think he or she would say?
- Have you ever flown under someone whom you felt was not as capable as you in flight skills and judgment?
- What is your management style in the cockpit?
- Have you ever worked for a female supervisor?
- What aircraft have you flown? Where to? Passengers? Cargo? What kind of engines did they have? What did you like and dislike about each aircraft? How much time do you have in each aircraft? In what seat?
- How many hours have you flown in the last six months?
- How much lost time have you had in the past two years?
- What are the systems capabilities and limitations of the most recent aircraft you have flown?
- What was the most serious in-flight emergency situation you have faced? What did you do? What was the outcome? Would you do it again? Tell me about an emergency which you handled very well. One which you didn't handle too well.
- Have you ever made a decision in error? What? Where? How? Why?

- Have you ever regretted the judgment you used in an aircraft?
- Have you ever been cited for a violation? Have you ever been involved in any flight-related accident or incident?
- What have you done in an aircraft which could have caused a problem?
- What was the dumbest thing you ever did in the air?
- Have you ever gotten into an argument with someone when you were in flight? Who? Where? Why? Outcome?
- What was the last disagreement you had with someone?
- When was the last time you lost your cool at work?
- What was your most stressful experience?
- What contact do you typically have with the ground crew and mechanics?
- What problems have you run into while flying?
- What type of pilots do you enjoy flying with? What type wouldn't you care to fly with?
- How was your relationship with subordinates, peers, and bosses?
- How do you handle constructive criticism?
- Tell me about your last performance review. Did you agree? If not, why not?
- Have you ever been turned down for a promotion? Why? Give me the details.
- Describe one of your recent typical flights/days.
- What airports have you flown into and out of?
- What has been your biggest thrill in flying?
- What was your most memorable flight? Worst flight?
- What was your most impressive performance experience? Your worst experience? From which did you learn the most?
- How do you feel about the management of your company? Who were your company's competitors?
- Which company have you enjoyed working for the most? Why?
- Have you ever been involuntarily terminated? Why? What were all the circumstances?

- Why did you leave each of your previous jobs? What are *all* the reasons? Why do you want to leave your present job? Is your company aware that you are interviewing with us?
- Is there anything you would like to discuss with us, or would like to add, modify, or delete from what you have told us before we contact your previous employers? Any problems we should know about? Can we contact your present employer and inquire about you?

MILITARY BACKGROUND

- Why did you decide to go the military route in obtaining your flight qualifications?
- How did you happen to choose the particular branch of military service you were in?
- What did you enjoy most about your military service? Least? What were the highlights? Why didn't you stay in and make it a career? Had you thought seriously about staying in?
- Who was the most impressive pilot you have flown with?
- Describe your last three assignments and commanding officers. What did you like most about each? Least?
- Describe the equipment you flew. Did you choose it? Why?
- Do you think fighter pilots or heavy transport pilots make the best airline pilots?
- Where have you flown?
- Describe your last fitness report.
- How long did it take you to upgrade? Why so long?
- Why should we consider an ex-military pilot over a civilian pilot?

CIVILIAN BACKGROUND

- Why weren't you in the military? Why didn't you choose

the military service to build your flight qualifications and experience?
- Who makes the best airline pilot—a military or civilian trained one? Why?
- If you had to do it over again, would you go the civilian or the military route?

EDUCATION

- Why didn't you complete college? Do you plan to?
- How did you happen to select the college/university you attended?
- How did you decide on your major?
- Why did you go on to get a Master degree in . . . (field)?
- What was your overall grade average? Why was it so low? How important do you think grades are? Does your grade average reflect your learning ability? In which courses did you make your best and poorest grades? Which courses gave you the most difficulty?
- Which courses did you enjoy most? Least? Which were the most flight related? Which have helped you the most? In what ways?
- Where there any courses you started but didn't finish? Any incompletes?
- What, if any, flight-related projects or term papers did you complete?
- Describe your best and worst professors.
- What percent of your college education and training did you pay for yourself? Did you work your way through college? What kinds of jobs?
- What are all the things you gained from your college education?
- If you were to do it over again, what changes would you make in the programs or courses you chose?

ROLE PLAYING

- Confronting situations involving you and your Captain, First Officer, Flight Attendants, ground crew, and passengers—how *you* would handle such incidents.
- What would you do if you were First Officer and your Captain "broke minimums"? What if you were the Flight Engineer and no corrective action was being taken?
- If you just completed a long day of flying in bad weather with a new Captain, what might you say that was positive to him?
- How would you handle a situation where your Captain didn't seem to like you or care to talk to you?
- What would you do if you were a new FE and your Captain approached you with what appears to be the smell of alcohol on his breath?
- As Captain, what critical elements might you brief a new First Officer on?
- How would you handle a situation where you are the Captain and the Senior Flight Attendant approaches you saying she or he is having difficulty handling a particular passenger? Why? What else could you do?
- If no one talked to you in the cockpit, what would you do to start a conversation? When should there be silence?

DOMICILES

- Do you plan to relocate or commute? How will you avoid the problems commuters face?
- Where would you prefer to be based? Why? What would be your least desirable domicile?
- How do you feel about living in . . . (city)? How would your family feel about living there?
- What are all the reasons why you would want to live here in . . . (city)? What do you know about our area?

- How do you feel about our cold winters and hot, humid summers?

DEREGULATION

- What affect do you think deregulation has had upon the airlines and pilots? In what ways?
- How has deregulation affected our airline?
- Do you think our industry is better off regulated or deregulated?
- Do you think we should be regulated again? Why?

SALARY

- How do you feel about two-tier pay structures/systems? Why?
- How will you be able to live on your first year's salary?
- Do you know our starting salary for an FE?
- What do you think is a reasonable salary for an airline pilot?
- How do you feel about profit sharing versus straight salary?

UNIONIZATION AND MANAGEMENT

- What are your feelings about pilot/management/union relationships? What do you think about their interactions in today's atmosphere?
- How do you feel about the seniority system?
- How do you feel about the situation at . . . (airline)?
- What did you think of the strike at . . . (airline)?
- Would you cross a picket line? Why?
- Are you aware that you will be required to join the . . . (union)?

NOISE ABATEMENT

- How do you feel about noise abatement?
- What progress do you feel the airlines have made in noise abatement? What more could be done?

AFFIRMATIVE ACTION

- Do you know what an Affirmative Action Program is?
- How do you feel about affirmative action programs?
- Have you ever had any problems when instructing or directing women or minorities?
- How would you feel about flying under a Captain who is a female, or a minority, or is younger than you?
- What if your Captain is a female, you are on a layover, the crew is socializing, and she asks you to dance— what would you do? [You are a new Flight Engineer.]

MEDICAL

- Tell me about whatever medical, emotional, and physical problems you have had.
- Do you smoke or drink? To what extent?
- Have you ever tried drugs? Have you ever had a drug problem? When? Have you ever smoked Marijuana? Not even once?
- How many times have you been hospitalized or treated by a physician? For what reasons? What was the outcome?
- When do you normally go to bed and wake up on your days off? What is the longest period of time you have gone without sleep. When? Where? Why? Do you have any trouble falling asleep?
- How do you feel about flying nights and sleeping days?

- How much lost time have you had in the past five years?
- Have you ever failed to quality for a First-Class FAA Medical? Why? When?
- Tell me about your family's medical history, starting with your grandparents. What health problems did they have? How long did they live? What did they die of?
- What do you do to keep yourself in good physical condition? On a daily basis?
- What are your eating habits? What kind of food do you eat?
- Have you ever had a weight problem? When? Tell me more about it.

CRIMINAL

- Have you ever been arrested and convicted? When? Where? For What? What were the circumstances?
- Is there anything else we should know about?
- Would you object to taking a polygraph test? Why?

MARITAL STATUS

- Are you single?
- Are you divorced?
- Are you dating?
- Are you a confirmed bachelor?
- Why have you remained single so long? Any plans for marriage? Raising a family?
- Is this your first marriage?

FAMILY BACKGROUND

- Tell me about your family. What do your parents, brothers, and sisters do for a living? Where do they live? Do your parents reside in the same area? To whom do you feel closest? Are your grandparents living?

- Is your wife/husband employed? What kind of work does your spouse do? Tell me about her/him. How does your spouse feel about your being a pilot and being away from home often? How do you spend your time together?
- Tell me about your children. How old are they? What are they like?
- Describe your childhood to me. Who disciplined you? How were you disciplined? Did you get along better with your mother or your father? Whom do you love most? Why?

FREE TIME

- How do you spend your free time when you are not working? Who do you spend it with? Where do you go?
- What do you enjoy doing most?
- What sports do you enjoy? Participate in any?
- Do you work on your own car?
- What hobbies and interests do you have?
- What social, community, or professional clubs and organizations do you belong to?
- What year and make of automobile do you drive? Why did you choose it? How has flying affected your driving habits? How has your driving record been?
- What do you like to read? What was the last book you read?

ACCOMPLISHMENTS AND DISAPPOINTMENTS

- What has been your biggest accomplishment in flying

and in your personal life? What others? What have you accomplished in the last year?

- What obstacles have you had to overcome in getting to where you are today? How did you do it?
- What is the toughest decision you have ever had to make?
- Give me examples of your leadership accomplishments.
- What new ideas or suggestions have you had toward improvements and cost savings for your employers?
- What has been your biggest disappointment? How has it affected your life?
- What was the most stressful period in your life? How did you handle it?

STRENGTHS AND WEAKNESSES

- What are all your strengths, assets, and strong points? Which are your strongest traits? What can you bring to us? What do you have going for yourself. What would your present supervisor say your strong points are?
- What are your weaknesses and areas in which you can improve? What are your greatest liabilities? What would your present supervisor say your weak points are?
- Are you mechanically inclined? What are your mechanical skills? Do you work on your own car?
- How would you rate yourself as a pilot from 1 to 10, with 10 being the highest? Why? How would you compare yourself with other pilots?
- What was the most recent criticism leveled at you? By whom? Why? What would your spouse or closest friend say is your biggest fault? What would your worst enemy say about you?
- How do you handle constructive criticism?

PERSONALITY AND CHARACTER

- How would you describe yourself? How would your supervisor, spouse, and closest friends describe you? What short-comings would they say you have? If you were to describe yourself or your personality in one word, what would that word be? Who are your closest friends? What are they like? What do they do?
- Whom do you most admire?
- When did you mature?
- How do you make decisions?
- What qualities can you offer us?
- What kind of people do you enjoy being around the most? Least?
- What do you enjoy doing the most? Least?
- What are your likes and dislikes?
- Do you gamble? How much? When? Where? With whom?
- Do you think flying is a risky business?
- What difficult situations have you experienced?
- What problems do you have? What do you worry about?
- What is the furthest thing back that you can remember?
- Do you make decisions logically or intuitively?
- Have you ever regretted any decisions you've made?
- Have you ever worked/flown with someone you couldn't stand?
- What makes you angry? Mad? Sad? Happy? Upset?
- When did you have your last argument with someone? What caused it? What are most of your arguments over? Who is usually involved? How do they usually end?
- How do you cope with stress?
- How do you feel about swearing?
- What are your feelings about divorce?
- What type of pilot do you enjoy flying with?
- What sort of cockpit atmosphere do you like? How do you fight boredom? How would you react to a Captain reading a newspaper during a trip?

- What is the most interesting thing that has happened to you in the last twelve months?
- What have you done to improve yourself? Planning to do?
- If you had your life to live over again, what changes would you make? What would you have done differently?
- What is "success" to you. Do you feel you are a success?

FUTURE

- Where do you see yourself five years from now?
- What are your future personal and career goals? How do you plan to achieve them? When do you think you will achieve them?
- What problems do you think the airlines will face in the future?
- What will you do if you are furloughed? How will you support yourself?
- What will you do if we don't hire you?

QUESTIONS FOR THEM

- Do you have any questions for us? In what areas?
- Is there anything else you would like to ask us?

WRAP UP

- Is there anything else we should know about you, or anything that you would like to add to what you have said before we wrap things up? Any last words?
- How do you think your interview went? Why? What brings you to that conclusion?
- Why should we hire you over all the other fine candidates whom we are considering?

- If we can get pilots with twice as much flying experience as you, why should we hire you over them?
- If we can get college graduates, why should we consider you?
- In summary, what can you offer us that is different from what the other candidates have to offer?
- How did you prepare for this interview?
- Do you belong to FAPA?
- Did anyone prep you for this interview? Any of our pilots?
- How much notice will you give your current employer if we hire you?
- How soon can you start?

WHY CERTAIN QUESTIONS
ARE REPEATED

There may be times when the person interviewing you repeats the same question, or another interviewer asks the same thing worded a little differently. This can be a deliberate part of the interview strategy, for various reasons.

It may serve as a test to see if you are being consistent in your answers. Does the interviewer think you are twisting the truth, or are unorganized, or are having difficulty understanding the questions. Are you?

One interviewer may not have been concentrating on your answer to the original question, or wasn't satisfied with your answer in some respect, or felt you didn't express yourself clearly in answering the original question. He or she may want to run it by you again.

Another interviewer might think you were half-guessing your first answer or that you actually knew the correct answer but, for one reason or another, couldn't think of the right answer at the time. This interviewer is giving you the benefit of a doubt. You are being given a second chance to score more points, and you should take advantage of the opportunity.

CHAPTER 17

WHERE YOU SCORE POINTS WITH INTERVIEWERS

Throughout the course of your interviews with the Employment Department, the Flight Department, the Medical Department, and the company's psychologist, you are continuously being assessed on traits and factors that are considered important in predicting pilot success. After the interviews are completed, you will have scored less points, the same number of points, or more points than the other pilot candidates who are competing with you for the upcoming flight training classes. Each factor or area of questioning will have a certain weighted value. The choice of factors and the weight placed upon them will vary from airline to airline. Some are formally and consciously chosen and weighed, others are subconsciously selected and evaluated. Either way, they all count in determining who will be chosen.

These traits and factors are, in essence, a direct reflection of the things we discussed in earlier chapters, which addressed what the airlines are looking for in a proficient pilot and impressive individual. Interviewers will be looking for and at them during the time they spend with you.

This chapter reviews some of the key areas that affect your success as a pilot applicant.

What about the length of the interview and, consequently, the amount of time you will have to score points? You may think that a short interview is the easiest to handle. This is not so! A short interview offers you a very limited number of opportunities to score points. The longer the interview, the more chances you have to recuperate from the weak or poor answers you may have given earlier.

In considering all the traits and factors important to the airlines, the one that is most important is your "image"; that is the impact you have upon people, especially in their earliest interactions with you. This could make the difference if you are in a close race with another candidate. How strong or weak is your image? How professional do you appear to people who meet you for the first time? Interviewers often reflect on the impression they got when they first met you. Did you convey a warm, lukewarm, or cold feeling? What was going through their minds while they were shaking hands with you and introducing themselves? What was their reaction to your facial expressions, smile, gesture, walk, pace, alertness, and early responses to their questions and comments? How did they also feel about the clothes you were wearing, your haircut, the condition of your teeth, your weight, and the sound of your voice? These are all part of that first image-making impression.

Your communication skills are also of vital importance. How well do you speak and write, in the interviewer's opinion, based on your performance during the interview and everything that you have presented in writing (resume, cover letter, entries on your Employment Application, etc.)? Do you appear clear and concise in expressing yourself? Are you often misunderstood? Do people enjoy conversing with you? What are the interviewer's thoughts on how you come across to others? Many research studies have found that people judge others by their body language, perhaps even more than their vocal messages. Your body movements may be more credible than the words you use in conveying the truth to those with whom you communicate.

Your overall point score, of course, also depends on the type and quality of the flight training you received. How thorough and extensive was it? What is the reputation of the program and school? You should point out these things to interviewers when questioned, or you may bring them out on your own initiative.

Additional technical factors considered are total flight time, type of aircraft flown relative to the type of aircraft that this airline flies, and the type of recent flying you have done. Beyond having the required ratings, to what extent are you working on obtaining additional advanced ratings, licenses and certificates?

What is your uncorrected vision? Can it be corrected to 20/20 in both eyes? If not, why not?

As for your physical condition, the interviewers will want to know what you are doing to keep in shape. Have you had any recent health problems that you have not reported to them?

With regard to your educational background, the more applicable this is to a Flight Officer career, the more points you will receive. Do you have a Bachelor or Associate degree? Is it from an accredited university/college? How is your major field of study related to flying? In what ways is it beneficial?

The interviewers will determine to what extent your experience is directly flight related. To what extent did you fly under conditions parallel or similar to those flown by airline pilots? How extensive were the routes? Was there any night flying? In what areas did you fly? Do you have flight or ground school instructor experience? Did it involve disciplined training? (This kind of training can be to your advantage.)

Your learning ability is also important. This includes your ability to absorb and effectively apply new information and training, judging by your past record of flight experience (job progression) and formal education and training (grades and scores). What is the depth and extent to which you provide impressive answers to the questions asked during the interview? Will you, in the interviewer's opinion, be able to successfully comprehend and complete all future training and recurrent training programs required by the company's Flight Department? Do you "catch on quickly" when given instructions?

Something that is difficult to measure but important to the interviewer is your "love of flying" and the degree to which you are totally committed to flying as a career. With the advent of two-tier pay systems and other innovative compensation methods in the airline industry, management is getting more concerned about employment longevity. They want a maximum return on their investment in new hires: pilots who will stay with their airline until retirement. You don't want to oversell your outside interests and abilities—the interviewer may get the idea that you would leave flying for another career if an attractive opportunity presented itself. Let them know that you intend to stay with them until you retire from flying.

How does your maturity rate with the interviewer? Are you 23 years old and act 30, or are you 33 years old but act 20? Do your voice level, speed, and control reflect a mature person? Do you appear too set in your ways? How calmly and quickly would you react in an emergency?

Other factors that interviewers look for are:

- The extent to which you display self-motivation and initiative.
- Whether you have ever come up with ideas that increase productivity or reduce costs.
- Your receptiveness to change and to the opinions of those who don't always agree with you.
- Your effectiveness in working with all types of people.
- How well you can handle stress and pressure.
- How safe a pilot you are.
- How loyal you will be to the airline.
- Your general attitude.
- Your potential for further advancement into the Captain's seat and possibly into a flight managerial position.
- Your potential to handle other positions if you were

to become medically disabled.

Your actions, comments, and answers to questions asked during your interview will, to a great extent, determine the score you receive on each of the above factors.

Here is an example of how you can exploit every opportunity that is presented during your interview. Suppose you just finished answering a question and the interviewer catches a quick glimpse of you while looking down at your Employment Application and says, "You look like you were going to say something—were you?" You might quickly re-think all the questions you were asked and if you forgot some important point(s) you reply "Yes, a little earlier you asked me about . . . (question area). I would like to add this to what I said . . . ." You can capitalize in the same manner at any time during the interview if you are asked if you care to make any comments. This kind of strategy allows you to add to your score important points that otherwise might be lost.

CHAPTER 18

SOME "DON'TS"

Most of this book offers you advise on what to expect and what to do during your pilot applicant interview. It is also very important for you to know what not to do during the interview, and the following tips are given to help you make the best possible impression.

- Don't initiate the opening or closing of your interview—this is the interviewer's job.
- Don't start off asking questions—this will come later.
- Don't answer a question with the first thing that pops into your head. You might wish you hadn't spoken so quickly after it's too late to rectify your mistake. Think about the question and your answer before responding.
- Don't give flip answers.
- Don't give brief, curt answers to questions unless it's appropriate.
- Don't interrupt an interviewer.
- Don't criticize another candidate.
- Don't ask questions that might stump the interviewer.
- Don't irritate or frustrate an interviewer by debating or arguing a point to prove your own point. You may

be right in what you have to say but wrong when it comes to tactfulness. There are always several ways to give an honest answer. Choose the one that will most satisfy the interviewer.

- Don't show any signs of hostility toward the interviewer no matter what he or she says.
- Don't try to "butter up" the interviewer.
- Don't look at your watch. The interviewer may think that you want to get it over with, and he or she may help that happen.
- Don't criticize a former employer.
- Don't act like an "I can do anything" person.
- Don't ask an interview panel member to repeat a question unless you absolutely have to.
- Don't slouch—sit up straight.
- Don't joke. Display a sense of humor but don't kid around.
- Don't apologize for what you don't have. Explain your plans to acquire it.
- Don't chew gum.
- Don't come in with dirt under your fingernails, nor with long fingernails.
- Don't wear sunglasses.
- Don't repeat the question to the interviewer before giving your answer. It is a tip-off that you are stalling for time to think of a good answer. It also reflects an unprofessional image. You should be prepared to give a well-thought out answer to any question you might be asked.
- Don't ask the interviewer how well you did in the interview.
- Don't play one airline against another if you have two job offers. You may end up with none.

CHAPTER 19

INTERVIEWER REACTIONS
TO APPLICANTS

The image that you project to airline interviewers has been stressed throughout this book, and by now you should be familiar with the best ways to present yourself as a pilot candidate. In addition to the advice and information already presented, this chapter offers some typical comments by interviewers, both positive and negative, about various applicants they encountered. By studying these off-the-record, random comments, you will gain further insight and clues that can affect your performance during interviews and earn you the highest possible score.

> Overall, I'm impressed . . . Presentation in general wasn't too good . . . Projects a good image . . . Seemed very frightened . . . Didn't seem to have any idea of the type of pilot we were looking for . . . Seemed very sincere.
> Had a weak handshake—felt like I was holding a dead fish . . . A handshake can never be too strong as far as I'm concerned . . . Now there is a firm handshake.
> Dressed well . . . He dressed too casual for the interview

... She was overdressed ... Suit was too tight on him and out of style ... Suit was too big on him ... Shoes weren't polished ... Shoes squeaked ... Socks were too short ... Wore an old tie ... Style and cut of his clothes made him look overweight ... Collar was too loose on him ... Everything worn looked brand new ... Dressed as well as any of our managers—looked very professional ... Clothes were wrinkled.

Wouldn't be embarrassed to introduce him to the president of our airline ... Doesn't look or act friendly ... Liked his smile.

She wore too much makeup ... Wears her makeup so well you wouldn't know she has it on ... Perfume was too strong.

Good eye contact ... Would look away every time I finished asking a question ... Kept dropping his head and looking down ... Wasn't afraid to look me straight in the eye ... When confronted, broke her eye contact with me ... Directed most of his eye contact to just one panel member ... Smiles with her eyes ... Has a critical look about him ... His eyes seemed to dart around the room throughout the interview.

Good posture ... Seems round shouldered and bent over ... Sat on the edge of the chair ... Looked stiff ... Looked like someone ready to be attacked—so I closed in ... His clenched hands looked like a boxer's fists ... His hands and feet looked glued together ... Never spoke with his hands or fingers ... Waved her hands and arms all over the place ... Seemed to constantly shift positions ... Never moved—looked like a manikin ... Kept tapping his fingers on the arm of the chair and his foot on the floor ... Held her hands together tightly as though she was hiding something in them ... Had a very nice professional image in all respects.

There was dirt under his nails ... Her nails were too long ... Must have a nail-biting problem—nothing left . . . Very clean-looking person . . . Hair didn't look combed . . . Needed to shave again . . . Moustache was too big and too bushy . . . Hair was too long . . . Looked very polished and trim.

Walked so slow that I had to slow down for him . . . Walked so fast he kept getting ahead of me.

Talks too fast . . . speaks so slowly, we'll never get around to covering all the questions . . . Talks a lot but doesn't say much . . . Could hardly hear him . . . Her voice kept cracking . . . Sounded like a teenager . . . Didn't articulate well . . . Would be a good public speaker . . . Mumbled . . . Words are choppy—not free flowing enough . . . Wouldn't trust him . . . Can you image having to listen to that during an entire trip . . . Can you picture a Captain speaking that way to a crew . . . Seemed awfully quiet . . . A loud person . . . Has poor timing . . . Comes on too strong . . . No self-confidence in his voice . . . Starts talking when she's not sure what she's going to say . . . Doesn't stop talking after he has made his point . . . His answers were well worded . . . Speaks and writes well . . . Seems hyper . . . Appears withdrawn.

A good listener . . . Was so concerned with his answers that he didn't really listen to our questions . . . Had to repeat my questions several times—wasn't listening closely . . . Seemed to know what we were looking for . . . Would pause to gather his thoughts before giving us an answer—good planning . . . Could hardly wait for us to finish the question—the impatient type . . . Interrupted me several times . . . Another smart-ass.

Gave good, meaty answers . . . Replies were too brief . . . Couldn't get more than a "yes" or "no" answer out of him . . . Some of her answers were fuzzy . . . Never seemed to get to the point . . . Too flip at times . . . Spoke in circles, repeating herself . . . Each reply was clearly stated and explained to our full satisfaction . . . Wasn't sure what point he was trying to make . . . We seemed to be on the same wavelength ... Would frequently respond with a question about the question I asked—felt as though he was interviewing me ... Not certain if he's just dense or is trying to pump us for clues to the answers we expect ... Would repeat my question before giving her answer, stalling for time to think of something to say.

Never really calmed down ... Seemed uptight throughout the interview ... So calm you would think he had met us before ... Sure couldn't shake him ... Had a lot of nervous energy ... Seemed to have trouble handling the stress of the interview itself—that concerns me.

Came on so defensive ... Was completely open ... Couldn't figure her out ... Too set in his ways ... Seemed biased at times ... Good sense of humor ... Didn't display any sense of humor ... Didn't try hard enough to sell himself.

Kept mispronouncing my name ... Kept forgetting my name ... Surprised he knew all our names and could match each face with each name.

Not assertive enough ... Too aggressive ... Too blunt and direct ... Not tactful ... Wouldn't take a stand on anything ... Replies too vague ... Seems arrogant ... Liked his approach.

Began getting too personal and informal with us ... Too formal ... Not very polite ... Never said thank you ... Not an appreciative person ... Really seemed to appreciate the opportunity to have an interview with us.

Appears to be a very demanding person—might be too rough on a crew if he were Captain ... Expects more in return for what he has to offer.

Flirted with our receptionist.

Kept calling me "Sir" throughout the entire interview—was starting to get on my nerves ... Never once addressed me as "Captain" or "Sir," nor by my last name—not too professional.

Kept quoting information from his Resume—we wanted

to hear it straight from him, in his own words.

Doesn't show much enthusiasm in wanting to fly for us
. . . Shows very little enthusiasm about anything . . .
Didn't know too much about us . . . Sure did a lot
of research on us . . . Convinced me he would rather
fly for us than anyone else . . . Have the feeling that
if we hired him and shortly afterwards he received
another job offer from a carrier he was most interested in, he would leave us for that carrier.

Tried to take over the interview at times.

Didn't seem prepared for the interview . . . Should have
anticipated more of the questions we asked . . . Did
her homework . . . Played it by ear throughout the
interview—wasted a lot of our time developing
answers which should have been thought out ahead
of time.

Can't quite buy why he didn't finish college . . . Didn't
satisfy me as to why she chose to major in that field
. . . All of his formal education is directly flight related
. . . I'm disappointed that his grade average is so
low . . . Never heard of that school—better check
out its accreditation . . . Wonder why she chose that
particular college . . . Didn't convince me that he
has committed himself to completing his degree
requirements . . . Appears to have gotten a lot out
of college.

Needs more multi-engine experience . . . Not enough
PIC time . . . Should have already completed his FE
Writtens . . . Didn't score well on the FE Writtens
. . . Considering that she doesn't have heavy flight
time and experience, she's very sharp . . . Question
her learning ability . . . Hasn't kept current . . . Should
have been more selective in who he flew for and the
equipment he chose to fly . . . Most of her total flight
time is in instructing . . . All of her experience is
concentrated in just in one area . . . Most of his
experience is "Single Pilot" . . . No experience in
heavy equipment . . . Never flew in our typical
weather conditions . . . Like his background—fits

in nicely with what we are looking for.

Can't see him as a Captain . . . Lacks self-confidence . . . Too lackadaisical . . . Too timid . . . Too forceful . . . Can't detect any strong leadership traits . . . Too impulsive . . . Not a decisive person . . . Seems insecure . . . Appears easily intimidated . . . Isn't team oriented . . . Can't see her as a "take charge" person . . . Will make a great future Captain . . . Like his attitude . . . Too critical of people . . . Lacks compassion . . . Tended to knock his company . . . Acted very uncomfortable when I asked why he hadn't made Captain yet . . . Believe he would be content being a professional Flight Engineer the remainder of his career.

Flies for prestige and salary—not a real love of flying . . . Didn't convince me he wasn't in flying mainly for the money . . . You couldn't buy her away from flying . . . You would think he was born a pilot . . . Bet he would quit us and go into another field within the next three years . . . Everything she has done seems related to flying in one way or another—she's hooked on it . . . Think his dad pressured him into becoming a pilot . . . Believe flying was his second career choice.

Not certain her husband wants her flying . . . His wife complained about his being away from home too frequently while he was in the military . . . Still quite uptight over the recent separation/divorce . . . Question his being able to do a good job for us and still raise two children on his own . . . Might be planning to fly for us for a few years, then leave to raise a family—wish she had said something to make me more comfortable that she wouldn't . . . He's engaged—wonder how his future wife feels about his work hours . . . Don't see any problems with the spouse . . . Seems as though there would be a conflict in their careers as far as required time and location commitments.

Has very few outside interests . . . Looks like a loner to me . . . Doesn't realize we're interested in the whole person—not just flight skills . . . Wonder what kind of an employee in general he would make . . . For someone who says he loves flying, doesn't keep up with what's going on in aviation . . . Isn't into sports at all . . . Seems very family oriented . . . Never mentioned his family—just talked about himself . . . Has very few hobbies . . . Doesn't belong to any organizations . . . Can't believe he could successfully continue running his side business and fly for us internationally . . . Has her mind on too many interests—doubt she will stay with us . . . Maintains a well-balanced career/personal life—has things under control.

Didn't ask any questions—expected at least one . . . Asked too many questions . . . Asked some very good questions . . . Questions he asked were centered around what we could do for him and not around us and where we are headed . . . Shouldn't have asked those questions—expected him to already know that information.

Feel he might have a lot of good answers in his head but he didn't bring them out during the interview—can't give him credit for what we didn't hear . . . Overstated his flight experience . . . Didn't give himself enough credit for what he has accomplished— should have sold himself more.

Didn't convince me as to why we should hire him over our other candidates . . . Tended to knock other pilot candidates rather than play up his own qualifications . . . Was doing well in the interview up to that point . . . Did a good job of summarizing what she had to offer our airline.

Should see and listen to himself on video tape, needs to improve his presentation . . . Has it all put together well.

You're Hired!

All of these paraphrased comments by interviewers point out how very important it is that you be thoroughly prepared for your interview, anticipating the questions that might be asked. Sit down and think out the positive answers you plan to give. Rank them in terms of those which would seem most meaningful and impressive to the interviewers. Give the most important first, the least important last. You have to "read the interviewer" well in order to determine how long he or she wants to listen to your answer. If you don't, you may be cut off by the interviewer with another question before you get to the really good stuff. Many pilot candidates have lost out to their competition by failing to follow this approach. They returned home with a lot of good answers which they didn't bring out in the interview because they didn't plan and organize what they were going to say. Don't let it happen to you.

It takes practice to develop tactful, smooth flowing correct answers. Go over several times in your mind the anticipated questions and best answers you can develop. Keep going over your presentation until it feels right to you and you are comfortable with all the words because they are the ones *you* use daily to express yourself. This system works—try it!

CHAPTER 20

WRAPPING UP THE INTERVIEW

The interviewers will decide when the interview will end. You will generally know that you are approaching the close of the interview when you are asked if you have any questions for them. You should have one or two questions related to their airline's future plans (new equipment, markets, etc.) and what they think you could do to further qualify yourself for their airline. The latter reflects the humility of a person who is well qualified but knows there is always room for improvement.

In the wrap up itself, you can expect to be asked why you think you should be hired over the other pilot candidates being interviewed. You can summarize your key strengths as they apply to your technical flight qualifications (ratings, time, aircraft flown, type of flying, training), formal education, and personal attributes. You might also be asked if you would like to make any further comments before you leave. If there is anything important that you forgot to cover earlier in the interview, this is the time to bring it to their attention.

It's important to thank the interviewers again for the opportunity to have presented your qualifications to them in person. If the atmosphere is appropriate, you may add that you feel confident you would make an excellent Flight Engineer, First Officer, and future Captain for their airline.

You should send a thank you letter to each of the key people whom you met. The theme of the letter should be: "Now that I have had the opportunity to meet you in person and visit your facilities, I am more impressed than ever with . . . (name of airline) and would greatly appreciate the opportunity to establish a long, successful flight career with your airline."

If the interviewers ask how you felt about the interview, be tactful by saying that you thought it was fair and thorough and you had tried to answer their questions to the best of your ability.

It is inappropriate to ask them what will happen next. They will let you know.

You should leave with a pleasant smile, a firm handshake, and a sincere "Thank you. I hope that I will have the opportunity to see you again."

CHAPTER 21

FINAL SELECTIONS

The pilots who are under final consideration will have the results of their testing, simulator check, medical, background investigation, and interviews reviewed by a selection team, consisting of two or more of the following people: Personnel Director, Employment Manager or Employment Interviewer, Head of the Flight Department, Flight Manager, Flight Training Manager, active or retired Captains, company physician, and psychiatrist or psychologist. When there are only a few people on the selection team, all the members must approve the candidate. When the selection team is large, one dissenting member could be overruled by the consenting members. A great deal depends on each member's status within the team and the importance of the factor in question that relates to the candidate's qualifications, presentation, or background verification.

If your employment, education, and training credentials don't check out, you won't be accepted. There must be confirmation by your past employers that you performed well. Neutral replies, as well as cases when the airline is unable to confirm a particular past employment, are considered negative.

The selection team will choose candidates to fill one or more of the upcoming training classes. You may be told that you have been selected while you are still at their facilities, or within a few days to two weeks by phone or express letter. Rejected applicants are sent a letter notifying them that other candidates were chosen, and that they can reapply in one year. You should not get discouraged and give up on the airlines if you were not selected. Someone else may have barely beaten you out of the running and it could have gone either way. It certainly does not mean that everyone who wasn't selected is unemployable. There have been a number of pilots who were not hired on the first go around, but were placed on hold and later reconsidered. It's advisable to write to the people who interviewed you and tell them that you will continue to build your flight and other qualifications toward matching every aspect of their particular pilot profile. You can state that you have your heart set on a flight career with them and are determined to succeed in fulfilling all of their requisites.

Airlines will not give out any information concerning the reasons why you were not selected, in order to avoid possible legal suits against their company by candidates who were not hired. The information is kept confidential.

"No thanks. I still haven't decided which offer to take."

A WORD OF CAUTION

In your quest to get your hands on all the written material you can find on interviewing techniques in preparation for upcoming airline interviews, you must be careful to avoid applying those techniques that could backfire.

Most books on how to present yourself in an interview were not written specifically for pilots seeking to advance their flight careers. The authors have never closely interacted with pilots, nor do they know the particular reasons why airlines decide to hire or turn down pilot candidates. These books often suggest the use of very aggressive interviewing techniques which may work well for an applicant who is applying for a sales representative or electrical engineer position and is not confronted with the very highly competitive labor market that pilots face. These same aggressive techniques applied by an applicant seeking an airline pilot's position could prove disastrous. The airlines are not going to bargain with an applicant on salary, position, geographic location, or other conditions of employment. Your primary objective as a Flight Officer job candidate is to sell yourself as a quality product, not to negotiate and bargain. You should be discriminating in choosing which techniques to use; some are suited to pilots, others are not. You may be taking unnecessary chances if you experiment with new techniques that have not been applied successfully by pilots. There is too much at stake for you to gamble.

IMPORTANT POINTS
TO REMEMBER

Airlines have found that they can generally attract all the technically well-qualified pilots they need. They can get the quantity they want; it is the quality candidate who is scarce. The applicant who successfully displays strong quality is very likely to be hired. Most of the pilots who haven't worked out well for the airlines are those who had problems interacting with people. The source of their problems seemed deep-seated in their attitude, personality, character, judgment, insight, lack of leadership, and professionalism—rather than in their flight skills and aircraft knowledge. It is these non-technical factors that interviewers want to sample and assess by listening to everything the candidate has to say and reviewing the results of psychological testing and background verifications and investigations.

Most airline pilot candidates spend too much of their life building their technical flight qualifications and not enough time selling themselves. If you do not openly express all the things you have going for yourself to the people who are interviewing you, how will they know that you possess these qualities? Display your enthusiasm in wanting to fly for them, your self-confidence, sincerity, objectiveness, and positive attitude. Interviewers believe that what they will get is what they see and hear. They don't accept the existence of anything that is invisible when it comes to applicant assessment.

You must make it clear that your main reason for being a pilot is your love of flying and not the money. Do not show a reluctance to accept a two-tier salary program, either in the comments you make or in the manner in which you make them. Your hesitation in giving a reply will be interpreted as a lack of acceptance of the two-level pay system.

You should state your willingness to also accept a seniority system if the airline is unionized. Interviewers who are Flight Managers and Captains have management's interests in mind when assessing candidates, but they are also members of the union representing the pilots. They are supportive of a seniority system tied in with performance as the prime criteria for upgrading Flight Officers. If the airline is not unionized, support the theory that there is no need for third party representation when management and the pilots have a good working relationship based upon fair and equitable employee treatment.

You should sound natural and spontaneous when answering questions, varying the speed of your replies and emphasis placed on important points. Try to flow with the tone of the interview. It's all right to pause after a question to show that you are gathering your thoughts and developing an appropriate answer—that's good planning. It's not good to appear programmed and well rehearsed. Of course, you should be prepared in advance for the questions you have anticipated, but your answers should not sound canned.

When answering any question you should state the most important points you have to make first. Before you do, however, you should listen carefully to the question to understand why it was asked, that is, the intent behind the question. You must make your important points first because you might not get the chance to make them if you wait until later in your reply. The interviewing schedule might not allow you the time. You could be cut off and denied the opportunity to fire your best shots.

Periods of silence during an interview can be stressful to an applicant. Interviewers will sometimes create such periods of silence during the interview in order to observe any signs that you are succumbing to stress. It's evident to the interviewer that you are under stress when you fidget in your chair, dart your eyes around the room, or begin talking. The thoughts of prolonged silence can be frightening to many people. Just sit quietly and wait for the next question. It's the interviewer's move, not yours. You should never display any irritation to the interviewer's using this technique or to anything else which may occur or be said during the interview.

It is your job to bring up all the things that you have going for you, rather than leaving something important unsaid. It will be beneficial if you can relate these things directly to the questions you are asked. If not, you must find opportunities to throw them in indirectly wherever they will fit, preferably in reply to a question that has some relevance to the point you wish to bring to their attention. The interviewer might give you an opportunity by asking "Is there anything else you would like to say?" Of course, it is appropriate for you to ask, "May I mention some other pertinent background that I have which supports my qualifications?" You should not be afraid of sounding conceited. The points you are making are not covered in your Employment Application or Resume. You create the opportunity to bring out as many as you possibly can. Work them into your answers even at the risk of overkill. You are more likely to strike out as a result of underkill than overkill. It is natural for people to become nervous in interviews and to forget to bring out points they planned to make. You should not be too concerned about having too much to say. It is overkill only when you spend all your time elaborating on one point when there are many other points to be made.

You can look at the interview from the perspective of a baseball game. The person at bat can hit the ball anywhere in the ball park, so all positions must be well covered if you are going to get the batter out. As the applicant, you must be prepared for different batters (the interviewers), different well hit balls (questions asked), to different areas of the field (topics covered). You don't want to lose the game because you failed to cover right field well.

You should not make excuses for what you don't have going for you. Play up your strengths and play down your weaknesses.

You can show your sense of humor, when appropriate, by going along with interviewers who kid one another or make a humorous remark about something that is said. Your smile or laugh will indicate that you are flowing with the tone of the interview. You can also inject humor into the conversation if it is directed to yourself. Of course, you don't want to force humor or make remarks that are not pertinent to the situation or that the interviewers would not understand.

You should cite examples wherever appropriate to reinforce and emphasize the points you are making in answering questions.

You should use the interviewer's name from time to time if you have good face-name recall and are astute at pronouncing names.

You should always be optimistic! You wouldn't have been called in for the interview in the first place if the airline didn't think that you met their flight qualifications. You must believe that you can sell yourself as well as you can build your flight time and ratings. You have complete control over the way you present yourself. As you learn various ways to improve your presentation your self-confidence will grow.

You should not waste valuable time worrying about your competition. This time is better spent on yourself preparing for your presentation.

Your goal should be to convince the interviewers that you are more interested in presenting what you can offer and do for their airline than in finding out what their airline can do for you.

You should consider taking advantage of opportunities to be interviewed by companies, even if you really don't want the job. The challenges of being interviewed are a learning experience that will increase your effectiveness as an applicant and, in turn, the chances of obtaining the job you really want.

It is good practice to conduct mock interviews until you are as calm as you can reasonably expect to be when facing the real thing. You can anticipate interview questions and determine in advance what you are going to say, speaking the words out loud, not just to yourself. It is easy to do great things in your mind. But when you have to do them in a real situation in the presence of others, you may have problems. The more prepared you are, the less nervous you will be. Fear feeds on inexperience and unprepared-ness. When you lose your composure while answering a question, you have blown it even though the answer itself (content) was good. No matter how astute you are in your flying skills and knowledge, if you can't perform well under the pressure of an interview, you won't be hired.

Your one and only goal is to get hired. No matter how strongly you would like to say things as you perceive them to be throughout the interview, you should not say them if they are going to rub the interviewers the wrong way. You must gear your responses to impress the person who asked the question. Remember that you are not talking to your friends or family, who may interpret everything you have to say in your favor. Interviewers want to select only the best candidates they can find. You may or may not be one of those candidates. So what if you think the interview is a game they play. If going along with their game is what it takes to get hired, then you can practice and prepare for that game to the very best of your ability.

The Flight Managers and Captains interviewing you must feel that they like you personally—enough to want to fly with you on trips. You may be together in the cockpit and on layovers for many hours. If there is something about your personality that bothers them, they would not want you as one of their crew members. Do everything you can to convey the image of a pleasant, friendly, thoughtful and sincere person who can get along with anyone.

At the close of the interview, come on with your best sales pitch. Everything you say should be positive with the assurance that you would make an excellent future Captain for them and you want the chance to prove it.

There are a few more points about your airline interviews that should be made. They relate to your mental and physical condition during this stressful moment in your life. It's a good idea to practice a few relaxation techniques the night before and the morning of your interviews. One recommended method is to sit in a comfortable chair and concentrate on completely relaxing your body in gradual steps, saying to yourself: "My toes are relaxing . . . now my feet . . . now my legs," continuing upward until your entire body is at ease. While in this state of complete concentration and relaxation, you can visualize your being interviewed and picture the interviewer asking you questions and hear yourself give impressive answers. This repeated exercise creates and reinforces positive images, reduces stress, and builds a feeling of self-confidence.

While you are driving to your interview, with the car windows rolled down, take several deep, long breaths . . . slowly inhale and exhale. Doing this repeatedly provides more oxygen to your brain. It will enable you to think more clearly and remain relatively calm during the interviews. This approach has been successfully taught at seminars to people who perform assignments under stressful conditions and must learn to relax and handle stress more effectively.

As a quick review, let's go over the key steps to a successful interview:

- Know the airline well
- Anticipate the questions
- Develop thorough answers
- Stay clam and in control of yourself
- Show your enthusiasm and self-confidence
- Sell yourself in every way you can

If what has been brought out in this book does nothing more than make you more self-confident, it is well worth the time you spent reading it. With more self-confidence, you will have considerably increased your chances of being hired. If you apply only half of what you have learned to your upcoming interviews, you can't help but increase your effectiveness. "Application" is the key word . . . you don't merely store this knowledge, you use it! If you picture yourself doing a good job, you will!.

The author sincerely hopes that what you have gained through reading this book will help you to land a job offer with your number one airline. Good Luck!

"I'm hired!"

"I'm hired!"

To schedule a mock pilot interview coaching session with Irv Jasinski, phone (619) 489-9419 between 9 a.m.- 6 p.m. (Pacific Coast Time) Monday-Friday.

INDEX

NOTES

NOTES